1½ STORY HOMES
Cape Cod • Georgian • Tudor • Contemporary Adaptations

HOME PLANNERS, INC.

Contents

Index to Designs

On the Cover: Cover design can be found on page 25.

How To Read Floor Plans and Blueprints

Selecting the most suitable house plan for your family is a matter of matching your needs, tastes, and life-style against the many designs we offer. When you study the floor plans in this issue, and the blueprints that you may subsequently order, remember that they are simply a two-dimensional representation of what will eventually be a three-dimensional reality.

Floor plans are easy to read. Rooms are clearly labeled, with dimensions given in feet and inches. Most symbols are logical and self-explanatory: The location of bathroom fixtures, planters, fireplaces, tile floors, cabinets and counters, sinks, appliances, closets, sloped or beamed ceilings will be obvious.

A blueprint, although much more detailed, is also easy to read; all it demands is concentration. The blueprints that we offer come in many large sheets, each one of which contains a different kind of information. One sheet contains foundation and excavation drawings, another has a precise plot plan. An elevations sheet deals with the exterior walls of the house; section drawings show precise dimensions, fittings, doors, windows, and roof structures. Our detailed floor plans give the construction information needed by your contractor. And each set of blueprints contains a lengthy materials list with size and quantities of all necessary components. Using this list, a contractor and suppliers can make a start at calculating costs for you.

When you first study a floor plan or blueprint, imagine that you are walking through the house. By mentally visualizing each room in three dimensions, you can transform the technical data and symbols into something more real.

Start at the front door. It's preferable to have a foyer or entrance hall in which to receive guests. A closet here is desirable; a powder room is a plus.

Look for good traffic circulation as you study the floor plan. You should not have to pass all the way through one main room to reach another. From the entrance area you should have direct access to the three principal areas of a house—the living, work, and sleeping zones. For example, a foyer might provide separate entrances to the living room, kitchen, patio, and a hallway or staircase leading to the bedrooms.

Study the layout of each zone. Most people expect the living room to be protected from cross traffic. The kitchen, on the other hand, should connect with the dining room—and perhaps also the utility room, basement, garage, patio or deck, or a secondary entrance. A homemaker whose workday centers in the kitchen may have special requirements: a window that faces the backyard or the view of the family room where children play; a gar

allows for a short trip with groceries; laundry facilities close at hand. Check for efficient placement of kitchen cabinets, counters, and appliances. Is there enough room in the kitchen for additional appliances, for eating in? Is there a dining nook?

Perhaps this part of the house contains a family room or a den/bedroom/office. It's advantageous to have a bathroom or powder room in this section.

As you study the plan, you may encounter a staircase, indicated by a group of parallel lines, the number of lines equaling the number of steps. Arrows labeled "up" mean that the staircase leads to a higher level, and those pointing down mean it leads to a lower one. Staircases in a split-level will have both up and down arrows on one staircase because two levels are depicted in one drawing and an extra level in another.

Notice the location of the stairways. Is too much floor space lost to them? Will you find yourself making too many trips?

Study the sleeping quarters. Are the bedrooms situated as you like? You may want the master bedroom near the kids, or you may want it as far away as possible. Is there at least one closet per person in each bedroom or a double one for a couple? Bathrooms should be convenient to each bedroom—if not adjoining, then with hallway access and on the same floor.

Once you are familiar with the relative positions of the rooms, look for such structural details as:

- Sufficient uninterrupted wall space for furniture arrangement.
- Adequate room dimensions.
- Potential heating or cooling problems—i.e., a room over a garage or next to the laundry.
- Window and door placement for good ventilation and natural light.
- Location of doorways—avoid having a basement staircase or a bathroom in view of the dining room.
- Adequate auxiliary space—closets, storage, bathrooms, countertops.
- Separation of activity areas. (Will noise from the recreation room disturb sleeping children or a parent at work?)

As you complete your mental walk through the house, bear in mind your family's long-range needs. A good house plan will allow for some adjustments now and additions in the future.

Each member of your family may find the listing of his, or exercise. Why not try it?

How To Choose a Contractor

A contractor is part craftsman, part businessman, and part magician. As the person who will transform your dreams and drawings into a finished house, he will be responsible for the final cost of the structure, for the quality of the workmanship, and for the solving of all problems that occur quite naturally in the course of construction. Choose him as carefully as you would a business partner, because for the next several months that will be his role in your life.

As soon as you have a building site and house plans, start looking for a contractor, even if you do not plan to break ground for several months. Finding one suitable to build your house can take time, and once you have found him, you will have to be worked into his schedule. Those who are good are in demand and, where the season is short, they are often scheduling work up to a year in advance.

There are two types of residential contractors: the construction company and the carpenter-builder, often called a general contractor. Each of these has its advantages and disadvantages.

The carpenter-builder works directly on the job as the field foreman. Because his background is that of a craftsman, his workmanship is probably good—but his paperwork may be slow or sloppy. His overhead—which you pay for—is less than that of a large construction company. However, if the job drags on for any reason, his interest may flag because your project is overlapping his next job and eroding his profits.

Construction companies handle several projects concurrently. They have an office staff to keep the paperwork moving and an army of subcontractors they know they can count on. Though you can be confident that they will meet deadlines, they may sacrifice workmanship in order to do so. Because they emphasize efficiency, they are less personal to work with than a general contractor. Many will not work with an individual unless he is represented by an architect. The company and the architect speak the same language; it requires far more time to deal directly with a homeowner.

To find a reliable contractor, start by asking friends who have built homes for recommendations. Check with local lumber yards and building supply outlets for names of possible candidates.

Once you have several names in hand, ask the Chamber of Commerce, Better Business Bureau, or local department of consumer affairs for any information they might have on each of them. Keep in mind that these watchdog organizations can give only the number of complaints filed; they cannot tell you what percent of those claims were valid. Remember, too, that a large-volume operation is logically going to have more complaints against it than will an independent contractor.

Set up an interview with each of the potential candidates. Find out what his specialty is—custom houses, development houses, remodeling, or office buildings. Ask each to take you into—not just to the site of—houses he has built. Ask to see projects that are complete as well as work in progress, emphasizing that you are interested in projects comparable to yours. A $300,000 dentist's office will give you little insight into a contractor's craftsmanship.

Ask each contractor for bank references from both his commercial bank and any other lender he has worked with. If he is in good financial standing, he should have no qualms about giving you this information. Also ask if he offers a warranty on his work. Most will give you a one-year warranty on the structure; some offer as much as a ten-year warranty.

Ask for references, even though no contractor will give you the name of a dissatisfied customer. While previous clients may be pleased with a contractor's work overall, they may, for example, have had to wait three months after they moved in before they had any closet doors. Ask about his follow-through. Did he clean up the building site, or did the owner have to dispose of the refuse? Ask about his business organization. Did the paperwork go smoothly, or was there a delay in hooking up the sewer because he forgot to apply for a permit?

Talk to each of the candidates about fees. Most work on a "cost plus" basis; that is, the basic cost of the project—materials, subcontractors' services, wages of those working directly on the project, but not office help—plus his fee. Some have a fixed fee; others work on a percentage of the basic cost. A fixed fee is usually better for you if you can get one. If a contractor works on a percentage, ask for a cost breakdown of his best estimate and keep very careful track as the work progresses. A crafty contractor can always use a cost overrun to his advantage when working on a percentage.

Do not be overly suspicious of a contractor who won't work on a fixed fee. One who is very good and in great demand may not be willing to do so. He may also refuse to submit a competitive bid.

If the top two or three candidates are willing to submit competitive bids, give each a copy of the plans and your specifications for materials. If they are not each working from the same guidelines, the competitive bids will be of little value. Give each the same deadline for turning in a bid; two or three weeks is a reasonable period of time. If you are willing to go with the lowest bid, make an appointment with all of them and open the envelopes in front of them.

If one bid is remarkably low, the contractor may have made an honest error in his estimate. Do not try to hold him to it if he wants to withdraw his bid. Forcing him to build at too low a price could be disastrous for both you and him.

Though the above method sounds very fair and orderly, it is not always the best approach, especially if you are inexperienced. You may want to review the bids with your architect, if you have one, or with your lender to discuss which to accept. They may not recommend the lowest. A low bid does not necessarily mean that you will get quality with economy.

If the bids are relatively close, the most important consideration may not be money at all. How easily you can talk with a contractor and whether or not he inspires confidence are very important considerations. Any sign of a personality conflict between you and a contractor should be weighed when making a decision.

Once you have financing, you can sign a contract with the builder. Most have their own contract forms, but it is advisable to have a lawyer draw one up or, at the very least, review the standard contract. This usually costs a small flat fee.

A good contract should include the following:
• Plans and sketches of the work to be done, subject to your approval.
• A list of materials, including quantity, brand names, style or serial numbers. (Do not permit any "or equal" clause that will allow the contractor to make substitutions.)
• The terms—who (you or the lender) pays whom and when.
• A production schedule.
• The contractor's certification of insurance for workmen's compensation, damage, and liability.
• A rider stating that all changes, whether or not they increase the cost, must be submitted and approved in writing.

Of course, this list represents the least a contract should include. Once you have signed it, your plans are on the way to becoming a home.

A frequently asked question is: "Should I become my own general contractor?" Unless you have knowledge of construction, material purchasing, and experience supervising subcontractors, we do not recommend this route.

How To Shop For Mortgage Money

Most people who are in the market for a new home spend months searching for the right house plan and building site. Ironically, these same people often invest very little time shopping for the money to finance their new home, though the majority will have to live with the terms of their mortgage for as long as they live in the house.

The fact is that all banks are not alike, nor are the loans that they offer—and banks are not the only financial institutions that lend money for housing. The amount of down payment, interest rate, and period of the mortgage are all, to some extent, negotiable.

• Lending practices vary from one city and state to another. If you are a first-time builder or are new to an area, it is wise to hire a real estate (not divorce or general practice) attorney to help you unravel the maze of your specific area's laws, ordinances, and customs.

• Before talking with lenders, write down all your questions. Take notes during the conversation so you can make accurate comparisons.

• Do not be intimidated by financial officers. Keep in mind that you *are not begging for money,* you are buying it. Do not hesitate to reveal what other institutions are offering; they may be challenged to meet or better the terms.

• Use whatever clout you have. If you or your family have been banking with the same firm for years, let them know that they could lose your business if you can get a better deal elsewhere.

• Know your credit rights. The law prohibits lenders from considering only the husband's income when determining eligibility, a practice that previously kept many people out of the housing market. If you are turned down for a loan, you have a right to see a summary of the credit report and change any errors in it.

A GUIDE TO LENDERS

Where can you turn for home financing? Here is a list of sources for you to approach:

Savings and loan associations are the best place to start because they write well over half the mortgages in the United States on dwellings that house from one to four families. They generally offer favorable interest rates, require lower down payments, and allow more time to pay off loans than do other banks.

Savings banks, sometimes called mutual savings banks, are your next best bet. Like savings and loan associations, much of their business is concentrated in home mortgages.

Commercial banks write mortgages as a sideline, and when money is tight many will not write mortgages at all. They do hold about 15 percent of the mortgages in the country, however, and when the market is right, they can be very competitive.

Mortgage banking companies use the money of private investors to write home loans. They do a brisk business in government-backed loans, which other banks are reluctant to handle because of the time and paperwork required.

Some credit unions are now allowed to grant mortgages. A few insurance companies, pension funds, unions, and fraternal organizations also offer mortgage money to their membership, often at terms more favorable than those available in the commercial marketplace.

A GUIDE TO MORTGAGES

The types of mortgages available are far more various than most potential home buyers realize.

Traditional Loans

Conventional home loans have a fixed interest rate and fixed monthly payments. About 80 percent of the mortgage money in the United States is lent in this manner. Made by private lending institutions, these fixed rate loans are available to anyone whom the bank officials consider a good credit risk. The interest rate depends on the prevailing market for money and is slightly negotiable if you are willing to put down a large down payment. Most down payments range from 15 to 33 percent.

You can borrow as much money as the lender believes you can afford to pay off over the negotiated period of time—usually 20 to 30 years. However, a 15 year mortgage can save you considerably and enable you to own your home in half the time. For example, a 30 year, $60,800 mortgage at 12% interest will have a monthly payment of $625.40 per month vs $729.72 per month for a 15 year loan at the same interest rate. At the end of 30 years you have paid $164,344 in interest vs $70,550 for the 15 year. Remember - this is only $104.32 more per month. Along with saving with a 15 year mortgage, additional savings

can be realized with a biweekly payment plan. So be sure to consult your borrowing institution for all of your options.

The FHA does not write loans; it insures them against default in order to encourage lenders to write loans for first-time buyers and people with limited incomes. The terms of these loans make them very attractive, and you may be allowed to take as long as 25 to 30 years to pay it off.

The down payment also is substantially lower with an FHA-backed loan. At present it is set at 3 percent of the first $25,000 and 5 percent of the remainder, up to the $75,300 limit. This means that a loan on a $75,300 house would require a $750 down payment on the first $25,000 plus $2,515 on the remainder, for a total down payment of $3,265. In contrast, the down payment for the same house financed with a conventional loan could run as high as $20,000.

Anyone may apply for an FHA-insured loan, but both the borrower and the house must qualify.

The VA guarantees loans for eligible veterans, and the husbands and wives of those who died while in the service or from a service-related disability. The VA guarantees up to 60 percent of the loan or $27,500, whichever is less. Like the FHA, the VA determines the appraised value of the house, though with a VA loan, you can borrow any amount up to the appraised value.

The Farmers Home Administration offers the only loans made directly by the government. Families with limited incomes in rural areas can qualify if the house is in a community of less than 10,000 people and is outside of a large metropolitan area; if their income is less than $18,000; and if they can prove that they do not qualify for a conventional loan.

For more information, write Farmers Home Administration, Department of Agriculture, Washington, D.C. 20250, or your local office.

New loan instruments

If you think that the escalating cost of housing has squeezed you out of the market, take a look at the following new types of mortgages.

The graduated payment mortgage features a monthly obligation that gradually increases over a negotiated period of time—usually five to ten years. Though the payments begin lower, they stabilize at a higher monthly rate than a standard fixed rate mortgage. Little or no equity is built in the first years, a disadvantage if you decide to sell early in the mortgage period.

These loans are aimed at young people who can anticipate income increases that will enable them to meet the escalating payments. The size of the down payment is about the same or slightly higher than for a conventional loan, but you can qualify with a lower income. As of last year, savings and loan associations can write these loans, and the FHA now insures five different types.

The flexible loan insurance program (FLIP) requires that part of the down payment, which is about the same as a conventional loan, be placed in a pledged savings account. During the first five years of the mortgage, funds are drawn from this account to supplement the lower monthly payments.

The deferred interest mortgage, another graduated program, allows you to pay a lower rate of interest during the first few years and a higher rate in the later years of the mortgage. If the house is sold, the borrower must pay back all the interest, often with a prepayment penalty. Both the FLIP and deferred interest loans are very new and not yet widely available.

The variable rate mortgage is most widely available in California, but its popularity is growing. This instrument features a fluctuating interest rate that is linked to an economic indicator—usually the lender's cost of obtaining funds for lending. To protect the consumer against a sudden and disastrous increase, regulations limit the amount that the interest rate can increase over a given period of time.

To make these loans attractive, lenders offer them without prepayment penalties and with "assumption" clauses that allow another buyer to assume your mortgage should you sell.

Flexible payment mortgages allow young people who can anticipate rising incomes to enter the housing market sooner. They pay only the interest during the first few years; then the mortgage is amortized and the payments go up. This is a valuable option only for those people who intend to keep their home for several years because no equity is built in the lower payment period.

The reverse annuity mortgage is targeted for older people who have fixed incomes. This new loan allows those who qualify to tap into the equity on their houses. The lender pays them each month and collects the loan when the house is sold or the owner dies.

CAPE COD DESIGNS . . . *dramatically capture the warmth and charm*

of an early period of our country's architectural history. The low profile of these 1½-story houses is the result of the necessity of the 17th-Century structures of Cape Cod to be able to withstand the lashing winds that frequently swept across the Cape. The Cape Cod house can be found in three recognizable types: The half house with two windows to one side of the front door; the three-quarter house with two windows to one side and one to the other; the full Cape with a center door flanked by two windows on either side. From these basic main structures, appendages were often added to accommodate the growing family.

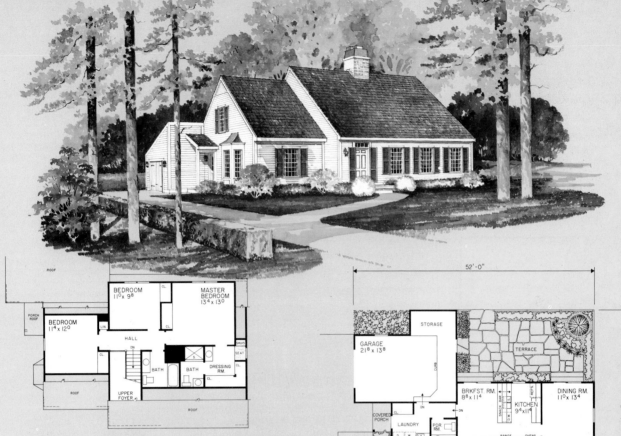

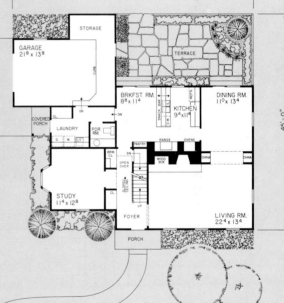

Design 122658 1,218 Sq. Ft. - First Floor
764 Sq. Ft. - Second Floor; 29,690 Cu. Ft.

● Traditional charm of yesteryear is exemplified delightfully in this one-and-a-half story home. The garage has been conveniently tucked away in the rear of the house which makes this design ideal for a corner lot. Interior livability has been planned for efficient living. The front living room is large and features a fireplace with wood box. The laundry area is accessible by way of both the garage and a side covered porch. Enter the rear terrace from both eating areas, the formal dining room and the informal breakfast room.

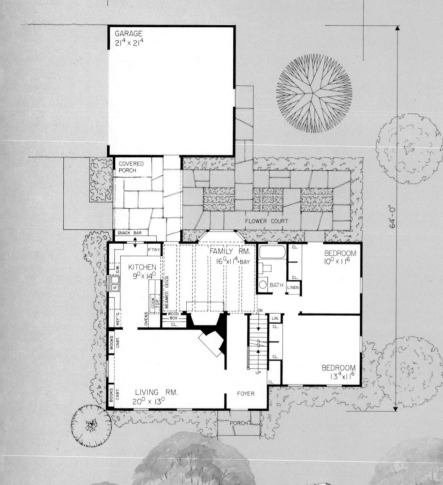

GARAGE
21⁴ x 21⁴

COVERED PORCH

SNACK BAR

FLOWER COURT

KITCHEN
9⁰ x 14⁰

FAMILY RM.
16⁰ x 11⁴ BAY

BEAMED CEIL'G

WOOD BOX

OVENS

COOK TOP

REF'G.

BOOKS

CABT.

BEDROOM
10⁰ x 11⁶

BATH

LINEN

P'TRY

CL.

BOOKS

CABT.

LIVING RM.
20⁰ x 13⁰

FOYER

BEDROOM
13⁴ x 11⁶

PORCH

44'-0"

64'-0"

Design 122145
1,182 Sq. Ft. - First Floor
708 Sq. Ft. - Second Floor
28,303 Cu. Ft.

● Historically referred to as a "half house", this authentic adaptation has its roots in the heritage of New England. With completion of the second floor, the growing family doubles their sleeping capacity. Notice that the overall width of the house is only 44 feet. Take note of the covered porch leading to the garage and the flower court.

MASTER BEDROOM
16⁰ x 13⁰-18⁴

WALK-IN CLOSET

DESK

BOOKS

PDR. RM.

BATH

CL.

LIN.

CLIPPED CEIL'G

STUDY/ BEDROOM
13⁴ x 11⁴

ROOF

ROOF

ROOF

DN

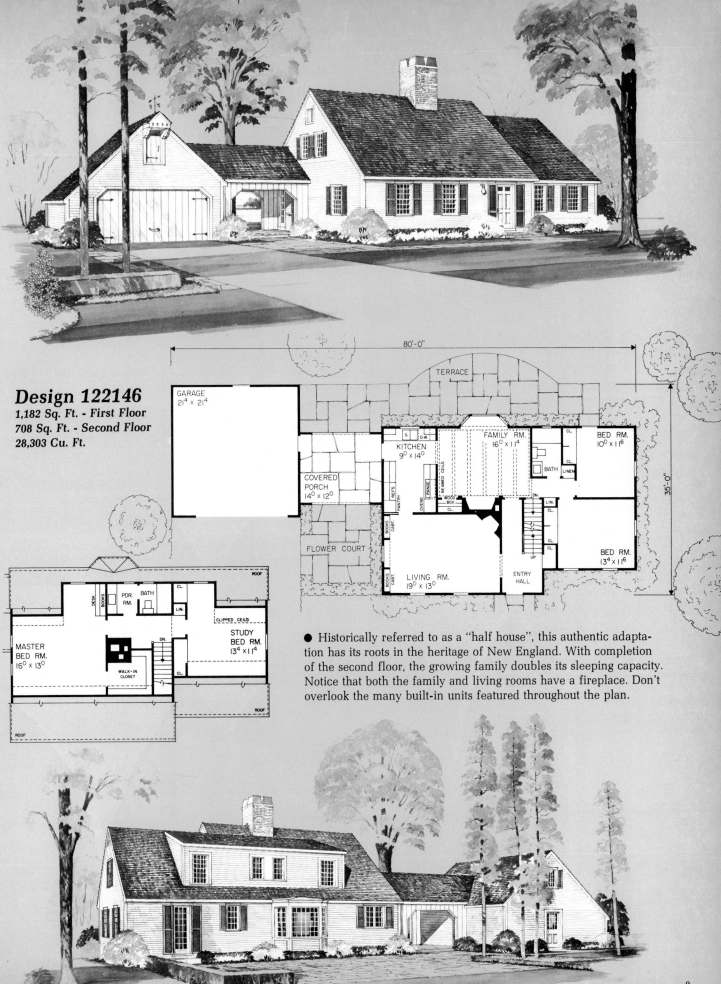

Design 122146

1,182 Sq. Ft. - First Floor
708 Sq. Ft. - Second Floor
28,303 Cu. Ft.

GARAGE
21⁴ x 21⁴

COVERED
PORCH
14⁰ x 12⁰

FLOWER COURT

80'-0"

TERRACE

KITCHEN
9⁰ x 14⁰

FAMILY RM.
16⁰ x 11⁴

BED RM.
10⁰ x 11⁶

BATH

LINEN

S. D.W.

CABT.

REFG.

PANTRY

OVENS

RANGE

WOOD
BOX

CL.

BOOKS

LIVING RM.
19⁰ x 13⁰

ENTRY
HALL

BED RM.
13⁴ x 11⁶

CL.

UP

35'-0"

CABT.

BOOKS

BEAMED CEIL'G

DESK

BOOKS

PDR.
RM.

BATH

CL.

LIN.

MASTER
BED RM.
16⁰ x 13⁰

WALK-IN
CLOSET

DN.

CLIPPED CEIL'G

STUDY
BED RM.
13⁴ x 11⁴

ROOF

ROOF

ROOF

● Historically referred to as a "half house", this authentic adaptation has its roots in the heritage of New England. With completion of the second floor, the growing family doubles its sleeping capacity. Notice that both the family and living rooms have a fireplace. Don't overlook the many built-in units featured throughout the plan.

Expanding the Half-House

Design 122682 976 Sq. Ft. - First Floor (Basic Plan)
1,230 Sq. Ft. - First Floor (Expanded Plan); 744 Sq. Ft. - Second Floor (Both Plans)
29,355 Cu. Ft. Basic Plan; 35,084 Cu. Ft. Expanded Plan

● Here is an expandable Colonial with a full measure of Cape Cod Charm. For those who wish to build the basic house, there is an abundance of low-budget livability. Twin fireplaces serve the formal living room and the informal country kitchen. Note the spaciousness of both areas. A dining room and powder room are also on the first floor of this basic plan. Upstairs three bedrooms and two full baths.

60'-0"

TERRACE

COVERED PORCH

DINING RM.
10⁸ x 12⁰

COUNTRY KITCHEN
20⁰ x 13⁰ - 15⁸

GARAGE
13⁸ x 20⁴

35'-0"

STUDY
13⁶ x 18⁰

PDR. RM.

FOYER

UP

BOOKS

LIVING RM.
20⁰ x 13⁰

PORCH

ATTIC STORAGE
(FUTURE ROOM)

ROOF

BEDROOM
12¹⁰ x 9⁸

BEDROOM
12¹⁰ x 9⁸

ROOF

LINEN

BATH

BATH

MASTER BEDROOM
11¹⁰ x 14⁰

ROOF

ROOF

● This expanded version of the basic house on the opposite page is equally as reminiscent of Cape Cod. Common in the 17th-Century was the addition of appendages to the main structure. This occurred as family size increased or finances improved. This version provides for the addition of wings to accommodate a large study and a garage. Utilizing the alcove behind the study results in a big, covered porch. Certainly a charming design whichever version you decide to build for your family.

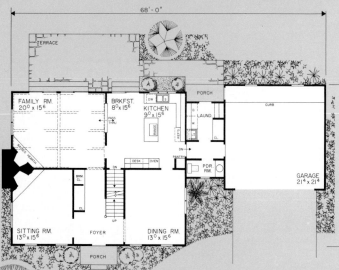

68'-0"

TERRACE

FAMILY RM.
20⁰ x 15⁶

BRKFST.
8⁰ x 15⁶

KITCHEN
9⁰ x 15⁶

PORCH

LAUND.

PASS THRU

PANTRY

PDR. RM.

DESK OVEN

BRM CL.

DN

UP

CL.

SITTING RM.
13⁰ x 15⁶

FOYER

DINING RM.
13⁰ x 15⁶

PORCH

CURB

GARAGE
21⁴ x 21⁴

31'-8"

Design 122644
1,349 Sq. Ft. - First Floor
836 Sq. Ft. - Second Floor
36,510 Cu. Ft.

ROOF

BEDROOM
11⁰ x 10⁶

BATH

LINEN

BATH

WALK-IN CLOSET

SHLVS

BEDROOM
17⁸ x 10⁶

DN

CL.

WALK-IN CLOSET

MASTER BEDROOM
13⁰ x 14⁸

ROOF

● What a delightful, compact, one-and-a-half story home. This design has many fine features tucked within its framework. The bowed roofline of this house stems from late 17th-Century architecture.

Design 122661
1,020 Sq. Ft. - First Floor
777 Sq. Ft. - Second Floor; 30,745 Cu. Ft.

● Any other starter house or retirement home couldn't have more charm than this design. Its compact frame houses a very livable plan. An outstanding feature of the first floor is the large country kitchen. Its fine attractions include a beamed ceiling, raised hearth fireplace, built-in window seat and a door leading to the outdoors. A living room is in the front of the plan and has another fireplace which shares the single chimney. The rear dormered second floor houses the sleeping and bath facilities.

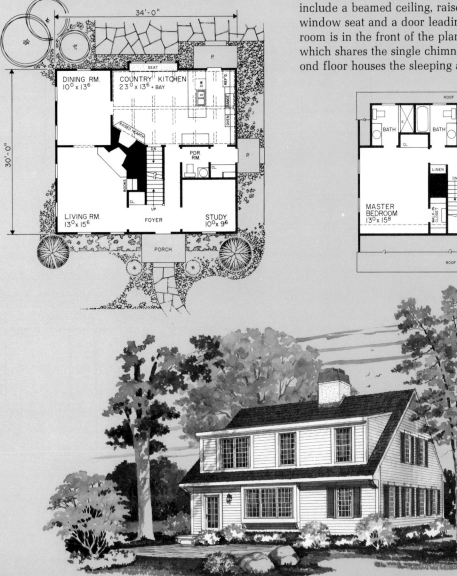

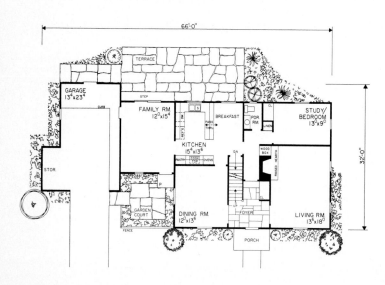

- Colonial charm could hardly be more appealingly captured than it is by this winsome design. List the features and study the living patterns.

Design 121901
1,200 Sq. Ft. - First Floor
744 Sq. Ft. - Second Floor; 27,822 Cu. Ft.

Design 121104
1,396 Sq. Ft. - First Floor
574 Sq. Ft. - Second Floor; 31,554 Cu. Ft.

- Here is a home whose front elevation makes one think of early New England. The frame exterior is highlighted by authentic double-hung windows with charming shutters. The attractive front entrance detail, flanked by the traditional side lites, and the projecting two-car garage with its appealing double doors are more exterior features.

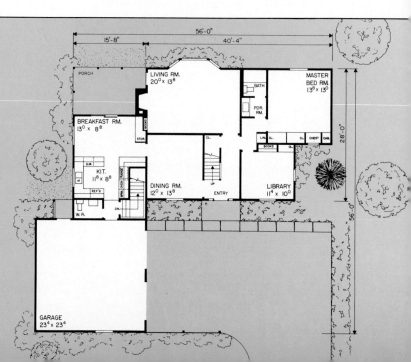

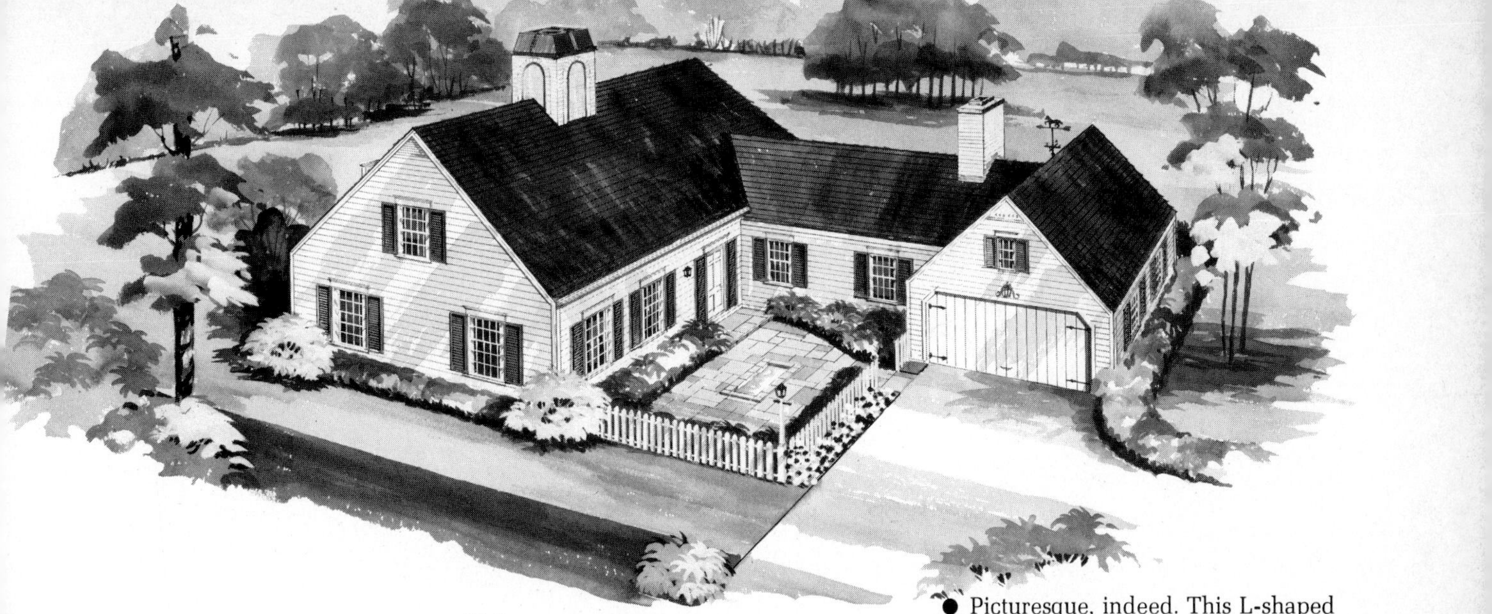

● Picturesque, indeed. This L-shaped one-and-a-half story home would attract its full share of attention even on Cape Cod. Study the excellent plan.

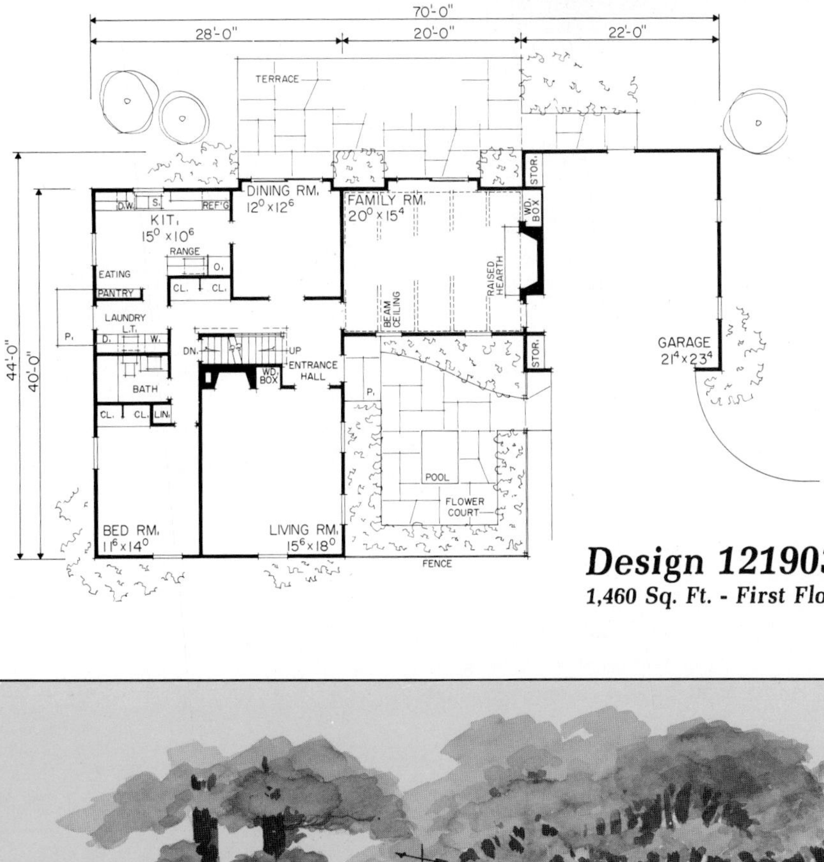
70'-0"
28'-0"
20'-0"
22'-0"
TERRACE
44'-0"
40'-0"
D.W.
S.
REF'G
KIT.
15⁰ x10⁶
RANGE
EATING
PANTRY
CL.
CL.
DINING RM.
12⁰ x12⁶
FAMILY RM.
20⁰ x15⁴
BEAM CEILING
RAISED HEARTH
WD. BOX
STOR.
LAUNDRY
D.
W.
BATH
CL.
CL.
LIN.
DN.
UP
ENTRANCE HALL
WD. BOX
STOR.
POOL
FLOWER COURT
GARAGE
21⁴x23⁴
BED RM.
11⁶x14⁰
LIVING RM.
15⁶x18⁰
FENCE

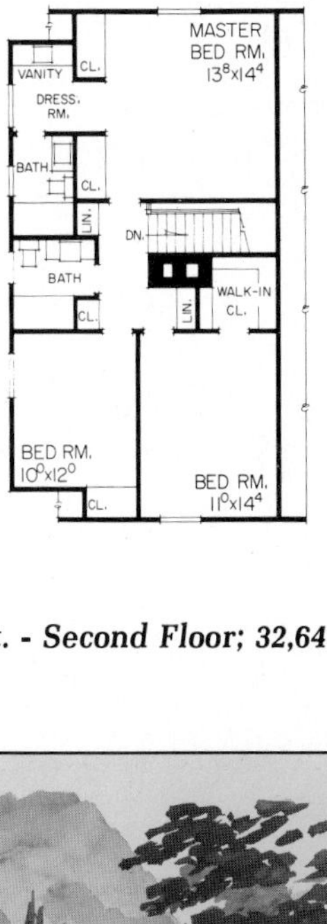
MASTER BED RM.
13⁸x14⁴
VANITY
CL.
DRESS. RM.
BATH
CL.
LIN.
DN.
BATH
CL.
LIN.
WALK-IN CL.
BED RM.
10⁰x12⁰
CL.
BED RM.
11⁰x14⁴

Design 121903

1,460 Sq. Ft. - First Floor; 854 Sq. Ft. - Second Floor; 32,647 Cu. Ft.

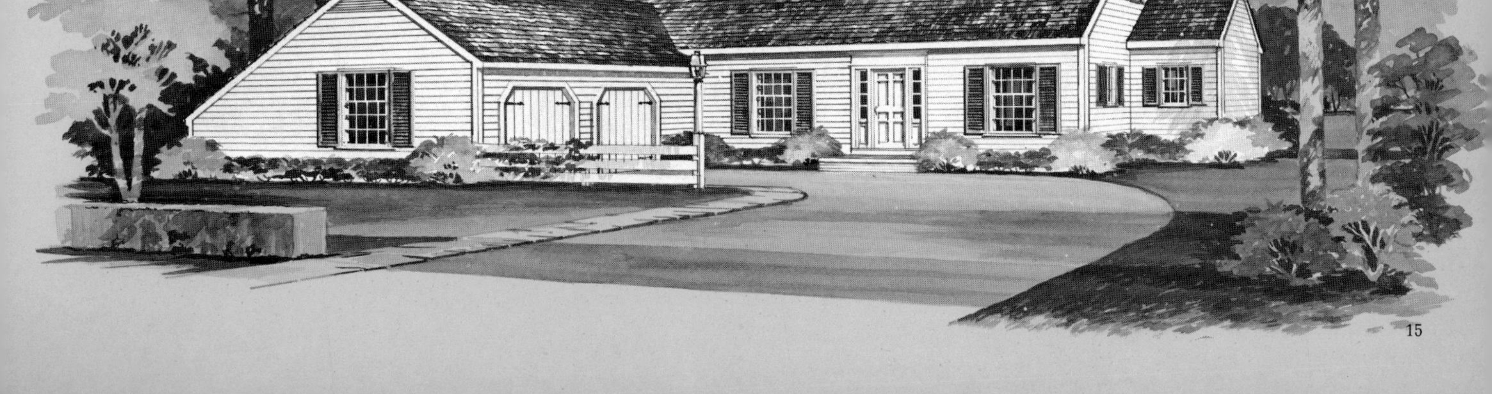

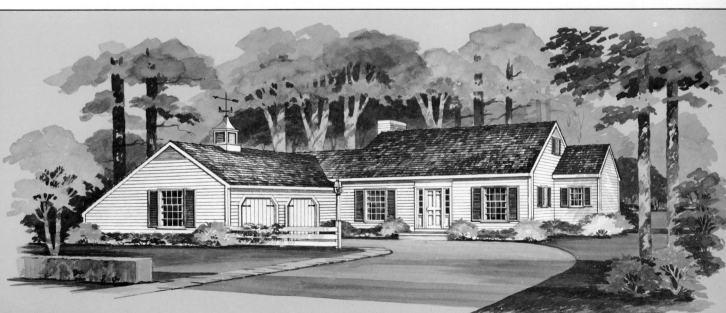

Design 122631

1,634 Sq. Ft. - First Floor
1,011 Sq. Ft. - Second Floor; 33,720 Cu. Ft.

● Two fireplaces and much more! Notice how all the rooms are accessible from the main hall. That keeps traffic in each room to a minimum, saving you work by preserving your furnishings. There's more. A large family room featuring a beamed ceiling, a fireplace with built-in wood box and double doors onto the terrace. An exceptional U-shaped kitchen is ready to serve you. It has an adjacent breakfast nook. Built-ins, too . . a desk, storage pantry, oven and range. Plus a first floor laundry close at hand.

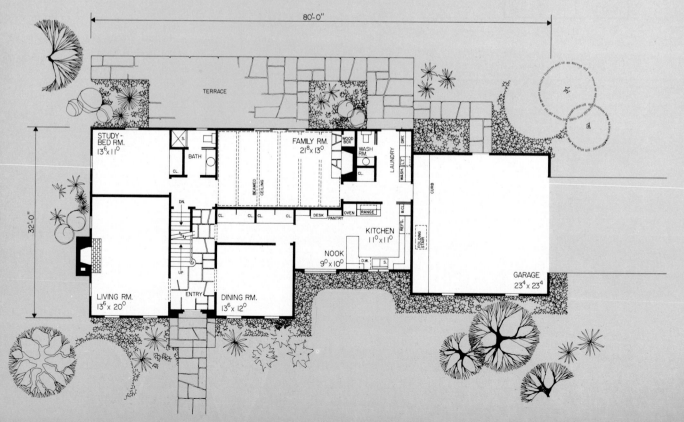

Design 121970

1,664 Sq. Ft. - First Floor
1,116 Sq. Ft. - Second Floor
41,912 Cu. Ft.

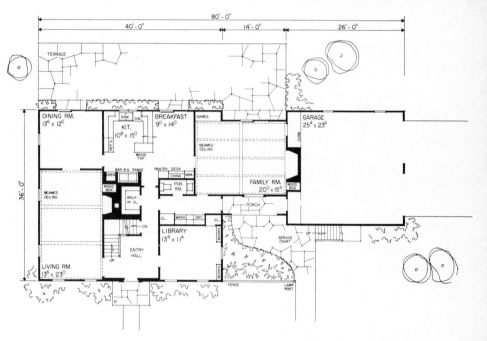

● The prototype of this Colonial house was an integral part of the 18th-Century New England landscape; the updated version is a welcome addition to any suburban scene. The main entry wing, patterned after a classic Cape Cod cottage design, is two stories high but has a pleasing groundhugging look. The steeply pitched roof, triple dormers, and a massive central chimney anchor the house firmly to its site. Entry elevation is symmetrically balanced; doorway, middle dormer, and chimney are in perfect alignment. The one story wing between the main house and the garage is a spacious, beam-ceilinged family room with splay-walled entry porch at the front elevation and sliding glass windows at the rear opening to terrace, which is the full length of the house.

Design 122563

1,500 Sq. Ft. - First Floor
690 Sq. Ft. - Second Floor; 38,243 Cu. Ft.

● You'll have all kinds of fun deciding just how your family will function in this dramatically expanded half-house. There is a lot of attic storage, too. Observe the three-car garage.

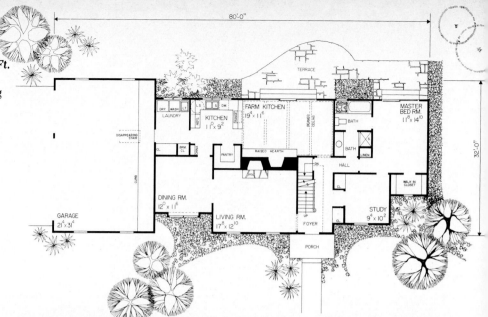

Design 122395

1,481 Sq. Ft. - First Floor
861 Sq. Ft. - Second Floor; 34,487 Cu. Ft.

● New England revisited. The appeal of this type of home is ageless. As for its livability, it will serve its occupants admirably for generations to come. With two bedrooms downstairs, you may want to finish off the second floor at a later date.

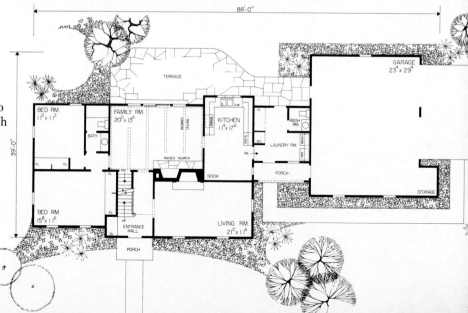

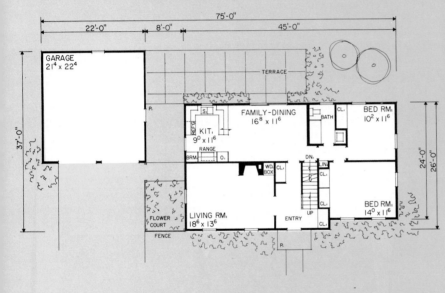

Design 123126 1,141 Sq. Ft. - First Floor
630 Sq. Ft. - Second Floor; 25,533 Cu. Ft.

● This New England adaptation has a lot to offer. There is the U-shaped kitchen, family-dining room, four bedrooms, two full baths, fireplace, covered porch and two-car garage. A delightful addition to any neighborhood.

Design 121791

1,157 Sq. Ft. - First Floor
875 Sq. Ft. - Second Floor; 27,790 Cu. Ft.

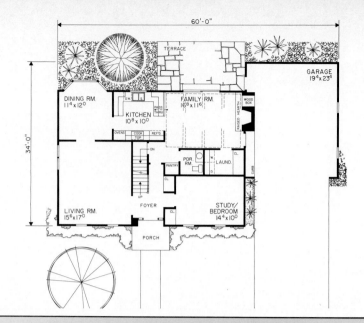

● Wherever you build this moderately sized house an aura of Cape Cod is sure to unfold. The symmetry is pleasing, indeed. The authentic center entrance seems to project a beckoning call.

Design 121870

1,136 Sq. Ft. - First Floor
936 Sq. Ft. - Second Floor; 26,312 Cu. Ft.

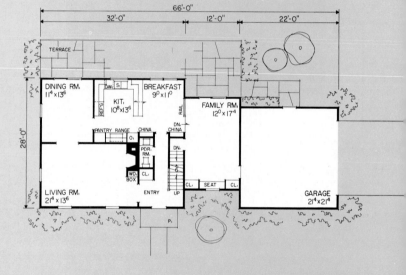

● Besides an enchanting exterior, this home has formal dining and living rooms, plus informal family and breakfast rooms. Built-ins are located in both of these informal rooms. U-shaped, the kitchen will efficiently service both of the dining areas. Study the sleeping facilities of the second floor.

Design 122396

1,616 Sq. Ft. - First Floor
993 Sq. Ft. - Second Floor; 30,583 Cu. Ft.

● Another picturesque facade right from the pages of our Colonial heritage. The authentic features are many. Don't miss the stairs to area over the garage.

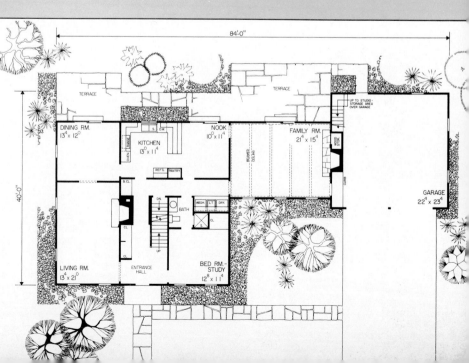

20

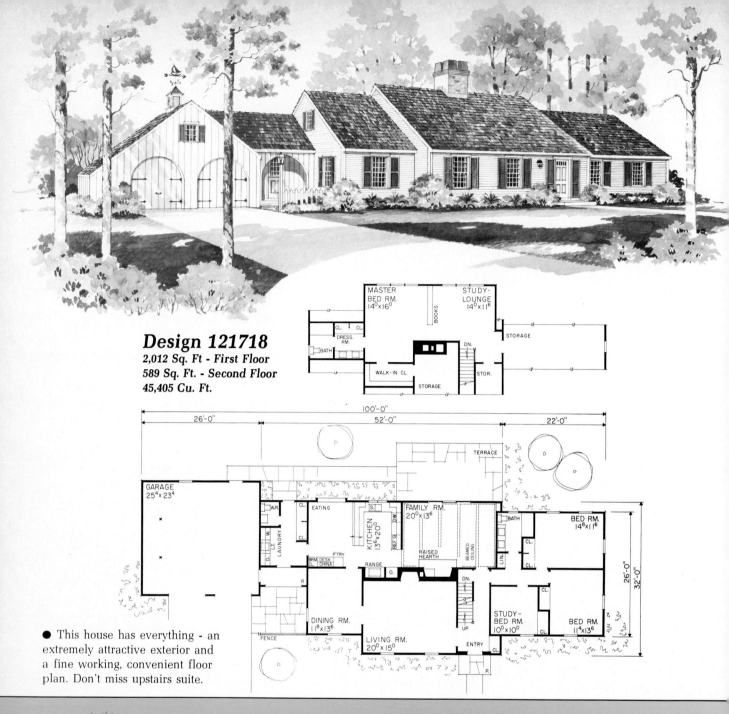

Design 121718

2,012 Sq. Ft - First Floor
589 Sq. Ft. - Second Floor
45,405 Cu. Ft.

MASTER BED RM. 14⁰x16⁰

STUDY-LOUNGE 14⁰x11⁶

BOOKS

CL. CL.

DRESS. RM.

STORAGE

BATH

DN.

WALK-IN CL.

STOR.

STORAGE

100'-0"

26'-0"   52'-0"   22'-0"

TERRACE

GARAGE 25⁴x23⁴

W.R.

CL.

EATING

S.

CL.

FAMILY RM. 20⁰x13⁶

BATH

BED RM. 14⁸x11⁶

D W

DI

LT

LAUNDRY

CL.

KITCHEN 13⁶x20⁰

REF'G.

DW

LIN.

CL.

CL.

P'TRY

RAISED HEARTH

BEAMED CEILING

26'-0"   32'-0"

BRM DESK CL CHINA

RANGE

O.

DN.

STUDY-BED RM. 10⁰x10⁰

CL.

P.

R

UP

CL.

BED RM. 11⁴x13⁶

DINING RM. 11⁸x13⁶

LIVING RM. 20⁰x15⁰

FENCE

ENTRY

CL.

P.

● This house has everything - an extremely attractive exterior and a fine working, convenient floor plan. Don't miss upstairs suite.

Design 121902 1,312 Sq. Ft. - First Floor
850 Sq. Ft. - Second Floor; 31,375 Cu. Ft.

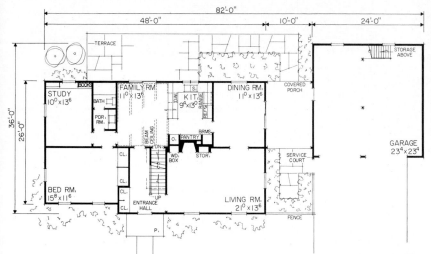

● This design has a great deal to offer the prospective home owner. The main living unit has a formal living room with fireplace and wood box, U-shaped kitchen with adjacent dining room, family room with beamed ceiling and sliding glass doors to the terrace, a study with built-in book shelves (or a second bedroom) and a bedroom. Later development of the second floor will create an additional two bedrooms and two full baths. This home offers a lot of livability and many years of enjoyable living.

Design 121987
1,632 Sq. Ft. - First Floor
980 Sq. Ft. - Second Floor
35,712 Cu. Ft.

● The comforts of home will be endless and enduring when experienced and enjoyed in this Colonial adaptation. What's your favorite feature?

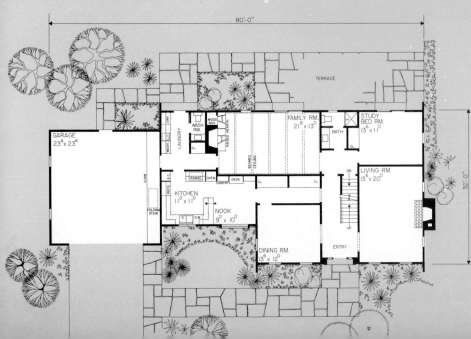

● Captivating as a New England village! From the weather vane atop the garage to the roofed side entry and paned windows, this home is perfectly detailed. Inside, there is a lot of living space. An exceptionally large family room which is more than 29' by 13' including a dining area. The adjoining kitchen has a laundry just steps away. Two formal rooms are in the front.

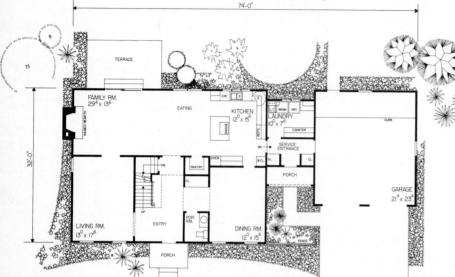

Design 122596
1,489 Sq. Ft. - First Floor
982 Sq. Ft. - Second Floor; 38,800 Cu. Ft.

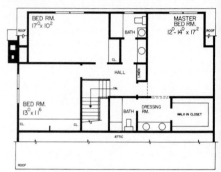

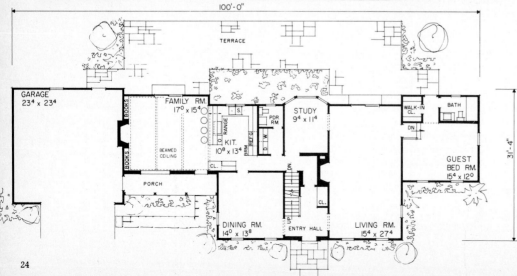

Design 121163
1,758 Sq. Ft. - First Floor
716 Sq. Ft. - Second Floor
34,747 Cu. Ft.

● The warmth of this exterior is characterized by the effective use of materials. The front entry hall routes traffic efficiently. Note the two fireplaces and study. Like so many one-and-a-half story designs, this home lends itself to building in stages. The guest bedroom may be made to function as the master bedroom, while leaving the completion of the second floor until a later date.

LOW BUDGET CHARM...

could hardly be better exemplified than by these delightful New England "cottages". In many cases, where a bedroom is located on the first floor, these designs can be built as expandable houses. Completion of the second floor at a later date allows for a most effective use of currently available funds. And, of course, these modest houses even with the attached garages generally do not require a large, expensive building site. Whether called upon to function as a young family's starter house, or to serve the growing family requiring expanding bedroom facilities, these houses deliver fine livability in a most cost-effective manner.

Design 122657 1,217 Sq. Ft. - First Floor
868 Sq. Ft. - Second Floor; 33,260 Cu. Ft.

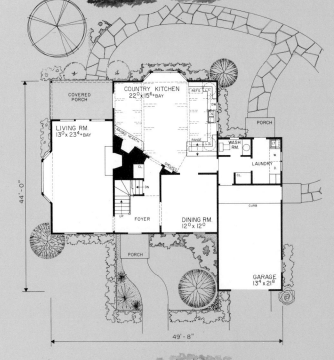

● Deriving its design from the traditional Cape Cod style, this facade features clap board siding, small-paned windows and a transom-lit entrance flanked by carriage lamps. A central chimney services two fireplaces, one in the country-kitchen and the other in the formal living room which is removed from the disturbing flow of traffic. The master suite is located to the left of the upstairs landing. A full bathroom services two additional bedrooms on the second floor.

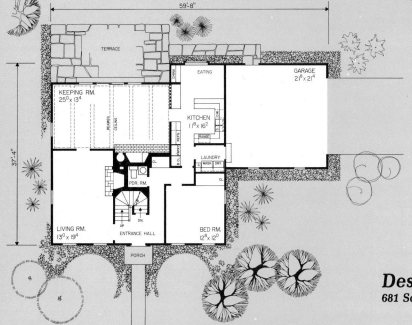

● From the island of Nantucket comes this unique 1¾-story cottage. This updated version of a style that was popular in the early 1700's has a charm all its own. The modern floor plan offers outstanding livability.

Design 122635
1,317 Sq. Ft. - First Floor
681 Sq. Ft. - Second Floor; 35,014 Cu. Ft.

● Another 1¾-story home - a type of house favored by many of Cape Cod's early whalers. The compact floor plan will be economical to build and surely an energy saver. An excellent house to finish-off in stages.

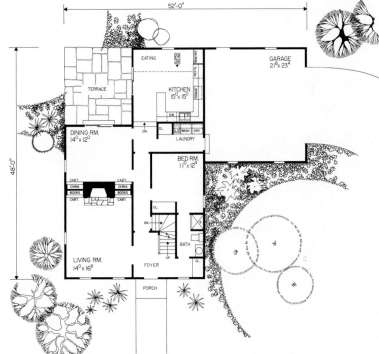

Design 122636
1,211 Sq. Ft. - First Floor
747 Sq. Ft. - Second Floor; 28,681 Cu. Ft.

Design 122569 1,102 Sq. Ft. - First Floor
764 Sq. Ft. - Second Floor; 29,600 Cu. Ft.

● What an enchanting updated version of the popular
Cape Cod cottage. There are facilities for both formal
and informal living pursuits. Note the spacious family
area, the formal dining/living room, the first floor laundry and the efficient kitchen. The second floor houses
the three bedrooms and two economically located baths.

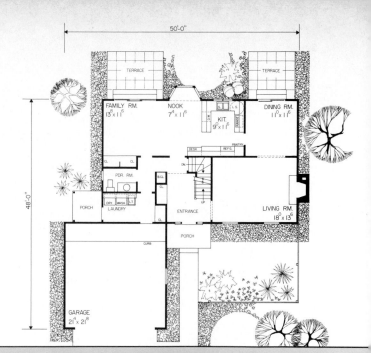

Design 122559 1,388 Sq. Ft. - First Floor
809 Sq. Ft. - Second Floor; 36,400 Cu. Ft.

● Imagine, a 26 foot living room with fireplace, a quiet study with built-in bookshelves
and excellent dining facilities. All of this,
plus much more, is within an appealing,
traditional exterior. Study the rest of this
plan and list its numerous features.

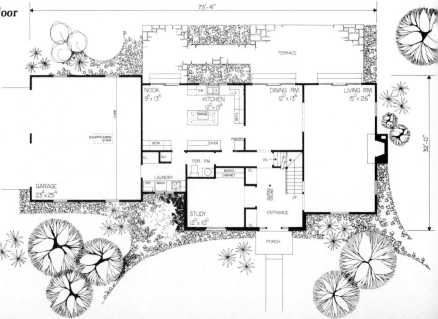

Design 121365 975 Sq. Ft. - First Floor
583 Sq. Ft. - Second Floor; 20,922 Cu. Ft.

● This cozy, story-and-a-half home will suit a small family nicely. Upon entering this home, you will find a good sized living room. A few steps away is the formal dining area which has an excellent view of the backyard. Adjacent is the nice sized kitchen. A bedroom, bath and a study with a built-in desk and bookshelves also will be found on this floor. There are two bedrooms upstairs and a full bath. This home is big on livability; light on your building budget.

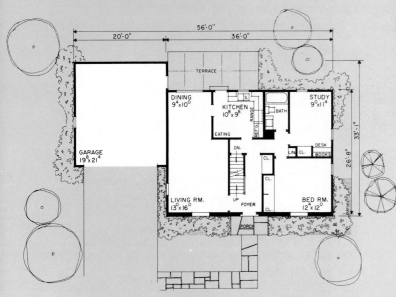

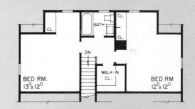

Design 122655
893 Sq. Ft. - First Floor
652 Sq. Ft. - Second Floor; 22,555 Cu. Ft.

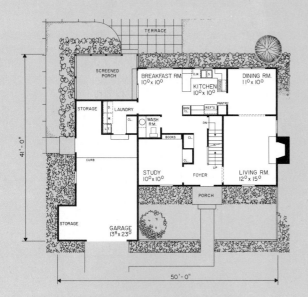

● Wonderful things can be enclosed in small packages. This is the case for this two-story design. The total square footage is a mere 1,545 square feet yet its features are many, indeed. Its exterior appeal is very eye-pleasing with horizontal lines and two second story dormers. Livability will be enjoyed in this plan. The front study is ideal for a quiet escape. Nearby is a powder room also convenient to the kitchen and breakfast room. Two bedrooms and two full baths are located on the second floor.

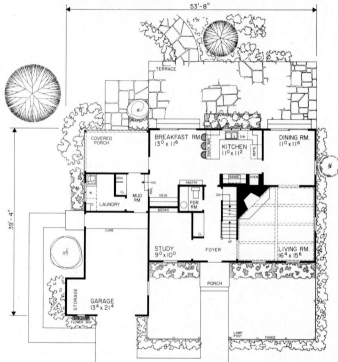

Design 122656 1,122 Sq. Ft. - First Floor
884 Sq. Ft. - Second Floor; 31,845 Cu. Ft.

● This charming Cape cottage possesses a great sense of shelter through its gambrel roof. Dormers at front and rear pierce the gambrel roof to provide generous, well-lit living space on the second floor which houses three bedrooms. This design's first floor layout is not far different from that of the Cape cottages of the 18th century. The large kitchen and adjoining dining room recall cottage keeping rooms both in function and in location at the rear of the house.

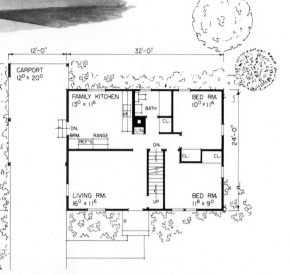

Design 121372
768 Sq. Ft. - First Floor
432 Sq. Ft. - Second Floor
17,280 Cu. Ft.

● Low cost livability could hardly ask for more. Here, is an enchanting exterior and a four bedroom floor plan. Note stairs to basement.

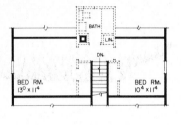

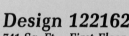

Design 122162
741 Sq. Ft. - First Floor
504 Sq. Ft. - Second Floor
17,895 Cu. Ft.

● This economical design delivers great exterior appeal and fine livability. In addition to kitchen eating space there is a separate dining room.

Design 121394

832 Sq. Ft. - First Floor
512 Sq. Ft. - Second Floor
19,385 Cu. Ft.

● The growing family with a restricted building budget will find this a great investment - a convenient living floor plan inside an attractive facade.

Design 122510

1,191 Sq. Ft. - First Floor
533 Sq. Ft. - Second Floor
27,500 Cu. Ft.

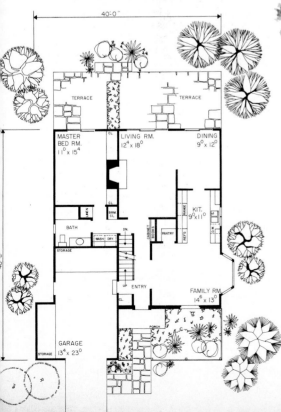

● The pleasant in-line kitchen is flanked by a separate dining room and a family room. The master bedroom is on the first floor with two more bedrooms upstairs.

33

Design 122852 919 Sq. Ft. - First Floor
535 Sq. Ft. - Second Floor; 24,450 Cu. Ft.

● Compact enough for even the smallest lot, this cozy design provides comfortable living space for a small family. At the heart of the plan is a spacious country kitchen. It features a cooking island - snack bar and a dining area that opens to a house-wide rear terrace. The nearby dining room also opens to the terrace. At the front of the plan is the living room, warmed by a fireplace. Across the centered foyer is a cozy study. Two second floor bedrooms are serviced by two baths. Note the first floor powder room and storage closet located next to the side entrance. This home will be a delight.

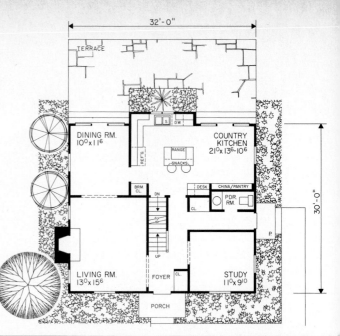

Design 122571 1,137 Sq. Ft. - First Floor
795 Sq. Ft. - Second Floor; 28,097 Cu. Ft.

● Cost-efficient space! That's the bonus with this attractive Cape Cod. Start in the living room. It is spacious and inviting with full-length paned windows. In the formal dining room, a bay window adds the appropriate touch. For more living space, a delightfully appointed family room. The efficient kitchen has a snack bar for casual meals. Three bedrooms are on the second floor.

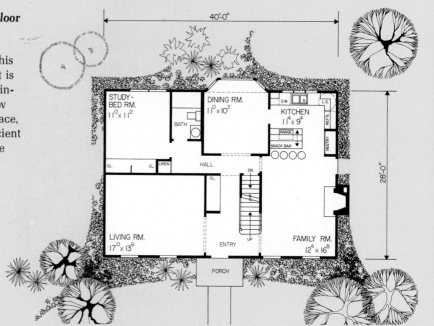

Design 123189 884 Sq. Ft. - First Floor
598 Sq. Ft. - Second Floor; 18,746 Cu. Ft.

● A large kitchen/dining area and living room are the living areas of this design. Four bedrooms, two up and two down, compose the sleeping zone. Each floor also has a full bath. A full basement and an attached garage will provide plenty of storage areas.

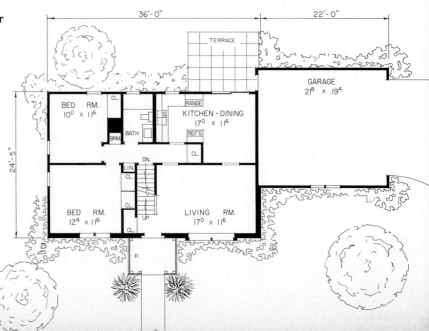

Design 122488

1,113 Sq. Ft. - First Floor
543 Sq. Ft. - Second Floor; 36,055 Cu. Ft.

● A cozy cottage for the young at heart! Whether called upon to serve the young, active family as a leisure-time retreat at the lake, or the retired couple as a quiet haven in later years, this charming design will perform well. As a year round second home, the upstairs with its two sizable bedrooms, full bath and lounge area, looking down into the gathering room below, will ideally accommodate the younger generation.

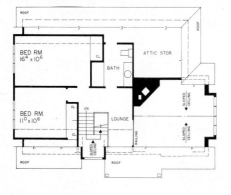

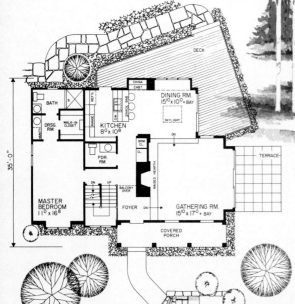

Design 122853

1,161 Sq. Ft. - First Floor
475 Sq. Ft. - Second Floor; 28,715 Cu. Ft.

● Natural stone, board-and-batten, multi-paned windows, overhanging eaves and the covered front porch highlight the exterior of this two-story home. Not only is the exterior well designed, but so is the interior. The sunken gathering room's ceiling is open to the second floor and is sloped for an even more dramatic appeal.

GEORGIAN & FARMHOUSE VERSIONS . . . *go well*

together here as they exemplify the formal graciousness of the Georgian facade versus the informal warmth of the front porch, farmhouse. The Georgian adptations are delightfully characterized by the symmetry of their window treatment, massive twin chimneys, dentil work at the cornices, and ornamented front entrance detailing. Greek columns are often a feature of these houses which may have either brick or frame exteriors. The more casual facades of the 1½-story farmhouses may have gable or gambrel roofs. Unadorned pillars support the sweeping front porches. Railings may or may not be present. Exceptional livability is the hallmark of these designs.

Design 122132
1,958 Sq. Ft. - First Floor
1,305 Sq. Ft. - Second Floor; 51,428 Cu. Ft.

● Another Georgian adaptation with a great heritage dating back to 18th-Century America. Exquisite and symmetrical detailing set the character of this impressive home. Don't overlook such features as the two fireplaces, the laundry, the beamed ceiling, the built-in china cabinets and the oversized garage.

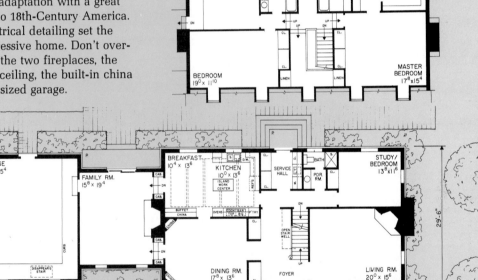

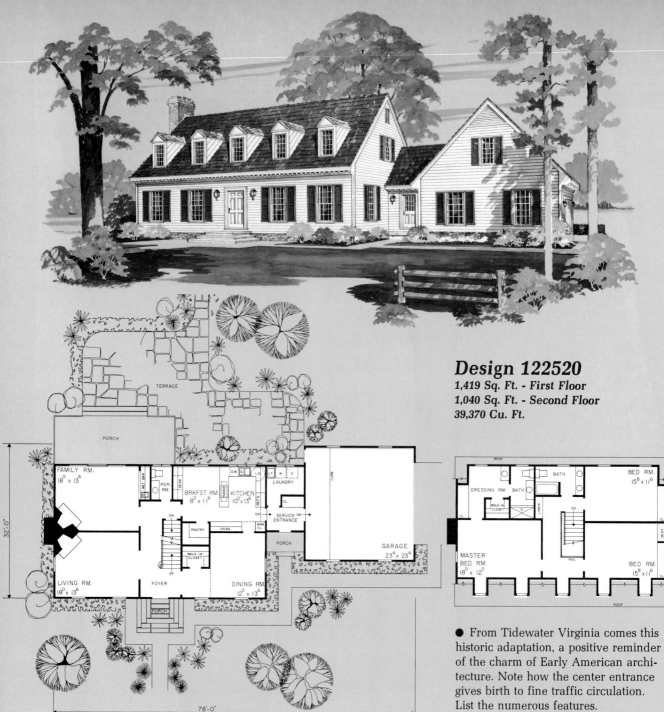

Design 122520

1,419 Sq. Ft. - First Floor
1,040 Sq. Ft. - Second Floor
39,370 Cu. Ft.

● From Tidewater Virginia comes this historic adaptation, a positive reminder of the charm of Early American architecture. Note how the center entrance gives birth to fine traffic circulation. List the numerous features.

Design 122684 1,600 Sq. Ft. - First Floor
1,498 Sq. Ft. - Second Floor; 47,395 Cu. Ft.

● Highlighting this plan is the spacious, country kitchen. Its features are many, indeed. Also worth a special note is the second floor studio/office. It is accessible by way of a staircase in the back of the plan. Just imagine the many uses for this area. There is a great deal of livability in this plan. Don't miss the three fireplaces or the first floor laundry.

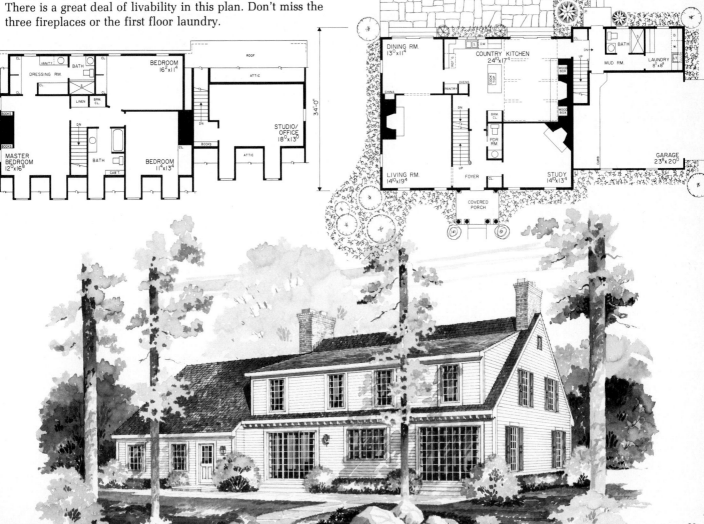

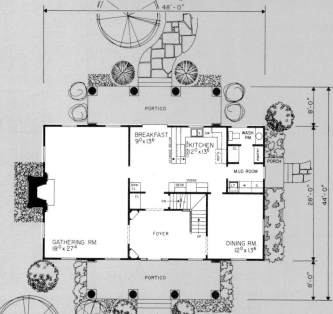

Design 122663 1,344 Sq. Ft. - First Floor
947 Sq. Ft. - Second Floor; 39,790 Cu. Ft.

● Reminiscent of the past, this home reflects the Greek Revival heritage. This is demonstrated in its front and rear porticoes which have graceful columns. While the exterior comes from yesteryear, the floor plan is designed to serve today's active family. Imagine the activities that can be enjoyed in the huge gathering room. It stretches from the front to the rear of the house. Three bedrooms are on the second floor.

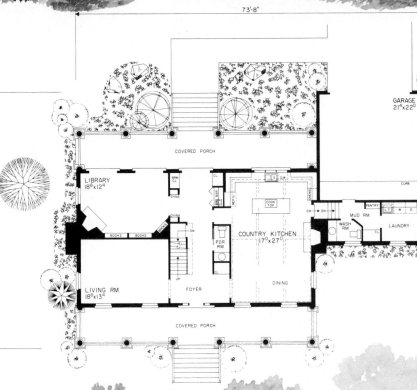

Design 122686

1,683 Sq. Ft. - First Floor
1,541 Sq. Ft. - Second Floor; 57,345 Cu. Ft.

● This design has its roots in the South and is referred to as a raised cottage. This adaptation has front and rear covered porches whose columns reflect a modified Greek Revival style. Flanking the center foyer are the formal living areas of the living room and library and the informal country kitchen.

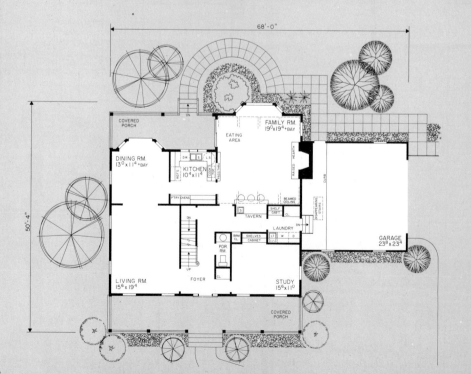

Design 122890
1,612 Sq. Ft. - First Floor
1,356 Sq. Ft. - Second Floor
47,010 Cu. Ft.

● An appealing Farm-house that is complimented by an inviting front porch. Many memorable summer evenings will be spent here. Entering this house, you will notice a nice-sized study to your right and spacious living room to the left. The adjacent dining room is enriched by an attractive bay window. Just a step away, an efficient kitchen will be found. Many family activities will be enjoyed in the large family room. The tavern/snack bar will make entertaining guests a joy. A powder room and laundry are also on the first floor. Upstairs you'll find a master bedroom suite featuring a bath with an oversized tub and shower and a dressing room. Also on this floor; two bedrooms, full bath and a large attic.

Design 122680
1,707 Sq. Ft. - First Floor
1,439 Sq. Ft. - Second Floor; 53,865 Cu. Ft.

● This Early American, Dutch Colonial not only has charm, but offers many fine features. The foyer allows easy access to all rooms on the first floor - excellent livability. Note the large country kitchen with beamed ceiling, fireplace and island cook top. A large, formal dining room and powder room are only a few steps away. A fireplace also will be found in the study and living room. The service area, mud room, wash room and laundry are tucked near the garage. Two bedrooms, full bath and master bedroom suite will be found on the second floor. A fourth bedroom and bath are accessible through the master bedroom or stairs in the service entrance.

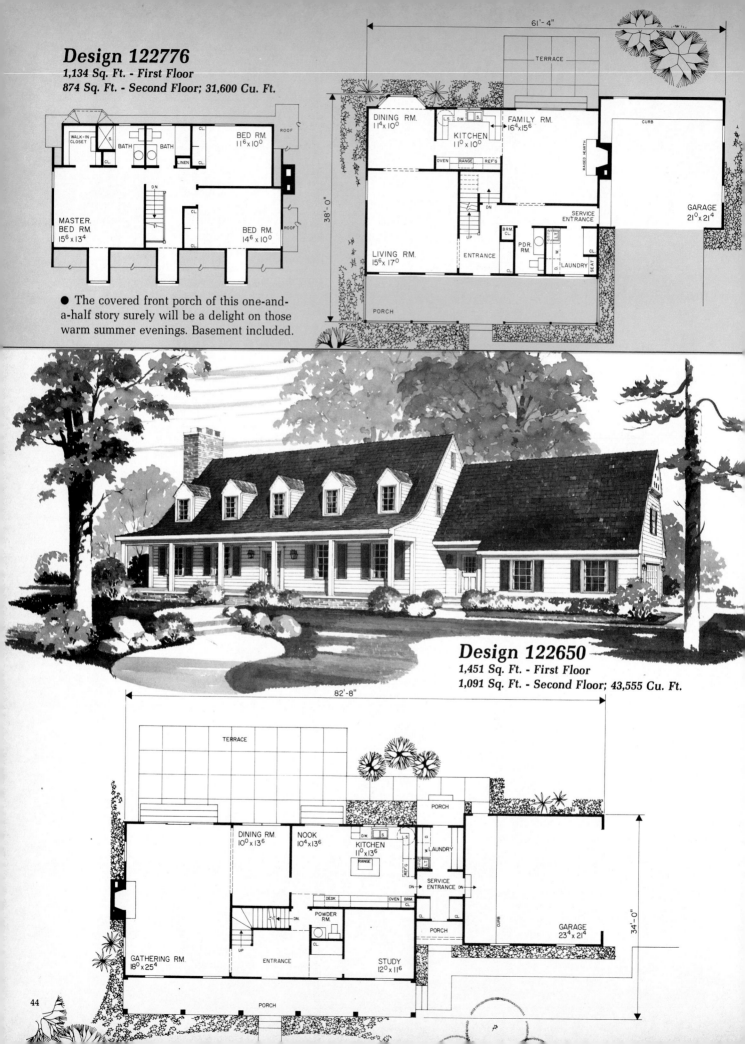

Design 122776

1,134 Sq. Ft. - First Floor
874 Sq. Ft. - Second Floor; 31,600 Cu. Ft.

WALK-IN CLOSET

BATH   BATH

CL.   LINEN   CL.

BED RM.
11⁶ x 10⁰

ROOF

DN

MASTER.
BED RM.
15⁶ x 13⁴

CL.

BED RM.
14⁶ x 10⁰

ROOF

● The covered front porch of this one-and-a-half story surely will be a delight on those warm summer evenings. Basement included.

61'- 4"

TERRACE

CURB

DINING RM.
11⁴ x 10⁰

KITCHEN
11⁰ x 10⁰

FAMILY RM.
16⁴ x 15⁶

OVEN   RANGE   REF'G

SERVICE ENTRANCE

GARAGE
21⁰ x 21⁴

RAISED HEARTH

38'-0"

DN

UP

BRM CL.

LIVING RM.
15⁶ x 17⁰

ENTRANCE

PDR. RM.

LAUNDRY

CL.

SEAT

PORCH

Design 122650

1,451 Sq. Ft. - First Floor
1,091 Sq. Ft. - Second Floor; 43,555 Cu. Ft.

82'-8"

TERRACE

PORCH

DINING RM.
10⁰ x 13⁶

NOOK
10⁴ x 13⁶

KITCHEN
11⁰ x 13⁶

LAUNDRY

SERVICE ENTRANCE

DN

RANGE

REF'G

DESK

OVEN   BRM CL.

GARAGE
23⁴ x 21⁴

CURB

34'-0"

DN

UP

POWDER RM.

CL.

GATHERING RM.
18⁰ x 25⁴

ENTRANCE

STUDY
12⁰ x 11⁶

PORCH

PORCH

MASTER BED RM. 18⁰ x 14¹⁰

WALK-IN CLOSET

DRESSING RM.

BATH

BED RM. 11⁴ x 10⁰

SHELVES

BATH

CL.

CL.

CL.

DN

LINEN

SHELVES

SHELVES

BED RM. 17⁰ x 12⁶

● The rear view of this design is just as appealing as the front. The dormers and the covered porch with pillars introduce this house to the on-lookers. Inside, the appeal is also outstanding. Note the size (18 x 25 foot) of the gathering room which is open to the dining room. Kitchen-nook area is very spacious and features a cooking island, built-in desk and more. Great convenience having the laundry and the service area close to the kitchen. Imagine, a fireplace in both the gathering room and the master bedroom! Make special note of the service entrance doors leading to both the front and back of the house.

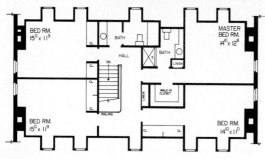

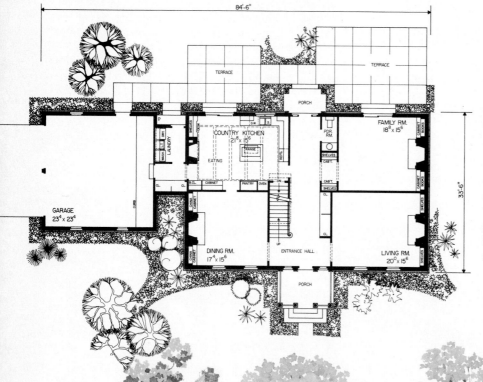

Design 122638
1,836 Sq. Ft. - First Floor
1,323 Sq. Ft. - Second Floor
57,923 Cu. Ft.

● The brick facade of this two-story represents the mid-18th-Century design concept. Examine its fine exterior. It has a steeply pitched roof which is broken by two large chimneys at each end and by pedimented dormers. Inside Georgian details lend elegance. Turned balusters and a curved banister ornament the formal staircase. Blueprints include details for both three and four bedroom options.

ENGLISH TUDOR STYLING . . . *adapts well to the*

1½-story type of house. In its many versions the low profile conjures pictures of the countryside of merrie olde England. The term, Tudor, has become a popularly accepted misnomer for what actually is more Elizabethan in character. It is this latter designation that historically identifies itself with half timbers, sculptured chimneys, stucco, diamond paned casement windows and high peaked roof lines. The enduring charm of the Cotswold Cottage has been captured by a couple of the following design adaptations. This selection of designs will have appeal to a full range of building budgets.

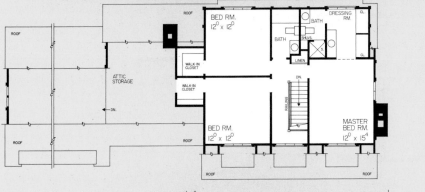

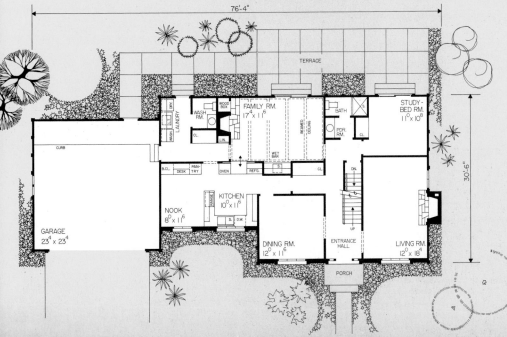

Design 122626

1,420 Sq. Ft. - First Floor
859 Sq. Ft. - Second Floor
34,974 Cu. Ft.

● This charming, one-and-a-half-story home elicits thoughts of an English countryside. It has a beckoning warmth that seems to foretell a friendly welcome. The exterior features are appealing, indeed. The window treatment, the stylish chimneys, the varying roof planes and the brick veneer and stucco exterior are among the distinguishing characteristics. Inside, the family living potential is outstanding. Notice the extra first floor bedroom with its adjacent full bath. The kitchen overlooks the front yard and is flanked by informal and formal dining areas. Nearby is the laundry and the convenient washroom. The family room, which functions with the rear terrace, will be the favorite gathering spot. Upstairs, a private bath and dressing room highlight the master bedroom. A second bath caters to the two large children's bedrooms.

47

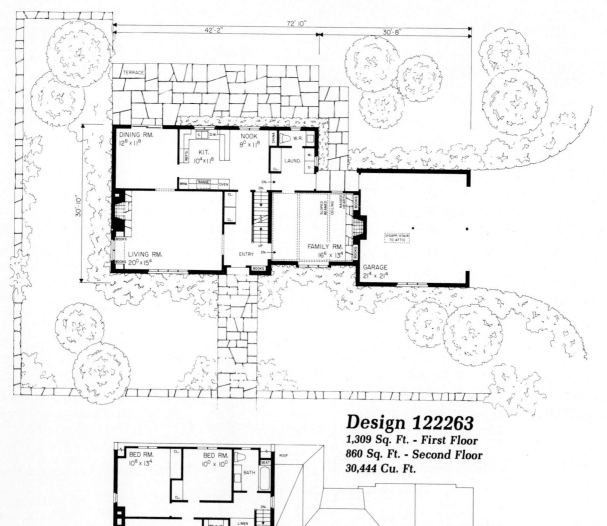

Design 122263

1,309 Sq. Ft. - First Floor
860 Sq. Ft. - Second Floor
30,444 Cu. Ft.

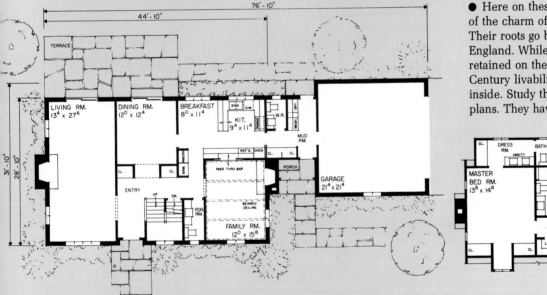

● Here on these two pages are examples of the charm of Cotswold architecture. Their roots go back to 17th-Century England. While the old world appeal is retained on the outside, the late 20th-Century livability is readily apparent inside. Study these exteriors and floor plans. They have much to offer.

Design 121990 1,412 Sq. Ft. - First Floor; 1,064 Sq. Ft. - Second Floor; 37,282 Cu. Ft.

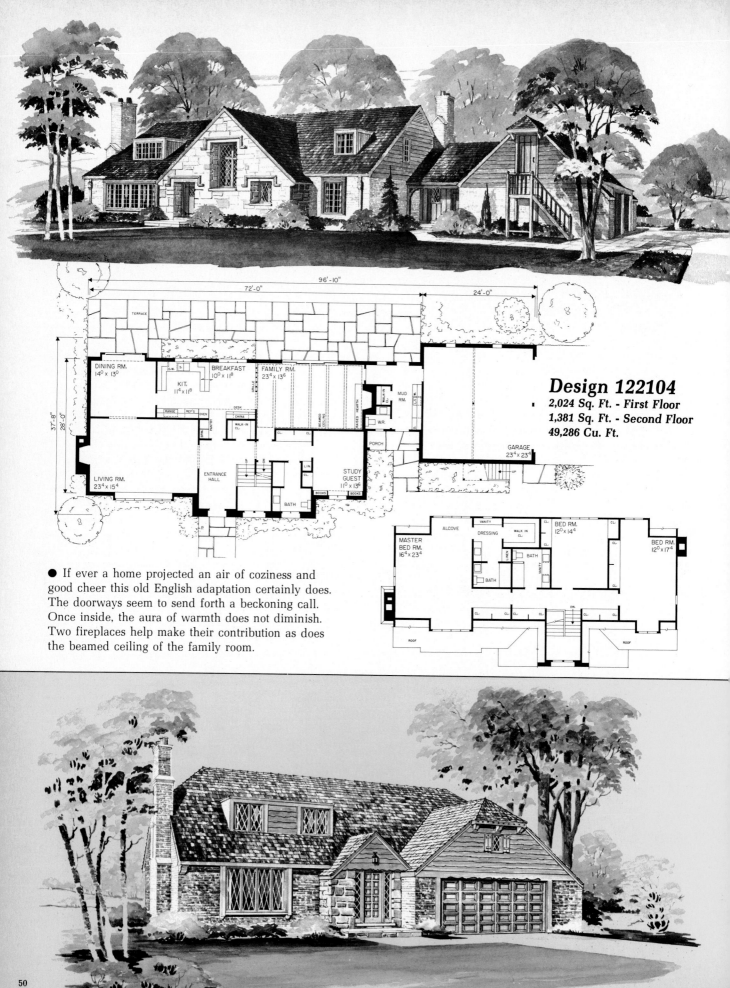

Design 122104

2,024 Sq. Ft. - First Floor
1,381 Sq. Ft. - Second Floor
49,286 Cu. Ft.

● If ever a home projected an air of coziness and good cheer this old English adaptation certainly does. The doorways seem to send forth a beckoning call. Once inside, the aura of warmth does not diminish. Two fireplaces help make their contribution as does the beamed ceiling of the family room.

Design 121991

1,262 Sq. Ft. - First Floor
1,108 Sq. Ft. - Second Floor
31,073 Cu. Ft.

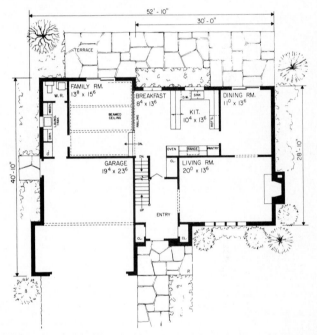

● Put yourself and your family in this English cottage adaptation and you'll all rejoice over your new home for many a year. The pride of owning and living in a home that is distinctive will be a constant source of satisfaction. Count the features that will serve your family well for years.

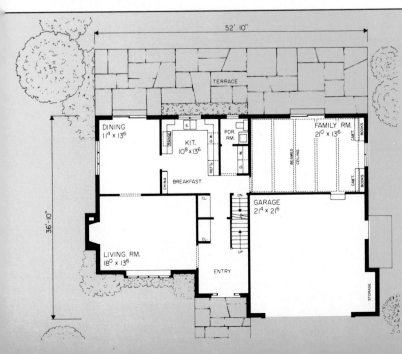

Design 122175 1,206 Sq. Ft. - First Floor

1,185 Sq. Ft. - Second Floor; 32,655 Cu. Ft.

● An English adaptation with all the amenities for gracious living. Note built-ins.

Design 122629

1,555 Sq. Ft. - First Floor
1,080 Sq. Ft. - Second Floor
38,479 Cu. Ft.

● This home will really be fun in which to live. In addition to the sizeable living, dining and family rooms, many extras will be found. There are two fireplaces one to serve each of the formal and the informal areas. The back porch is a delightful extra. It will be great to relax in after a long hard day. Note two half baths on the first floor and two full baths on the second floor to serve the three bedrooms. Count the number of closets in the spacious upstairs. The door from the bedroom leads to storage over garage.

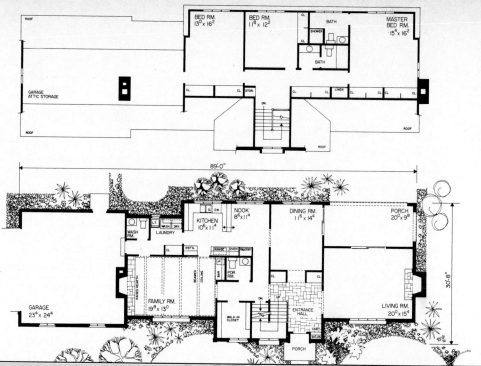

Design 122630

1,491 Sq. Ft. - First Floor
788 Sq. Ft. - Second Floor; 35,575 Cu. Ft.

● This distinctive version of Tudor styling will foster many years of prideful ownership and unique, yet practical living patterns. The main portion of the facade is delightfully symmetrical. Inside, the family living will focus on the 29 foot great room with its dramatic fireplace and beamed ceiling. The kitchen is outstanding with snack bar and dining nook nearby. Note the three large bedrooms each having its own dressing room. Extra storage space is available above the garage or may be developed into another room. Oversized garage includes a built-in workbench. Study plan carefully. It has much to offer.

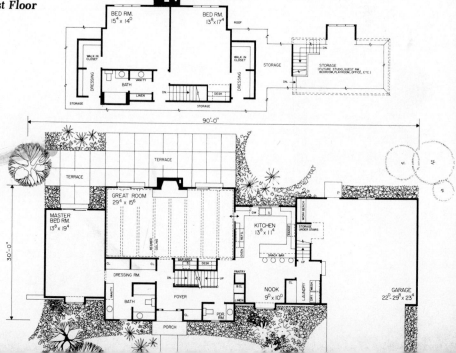

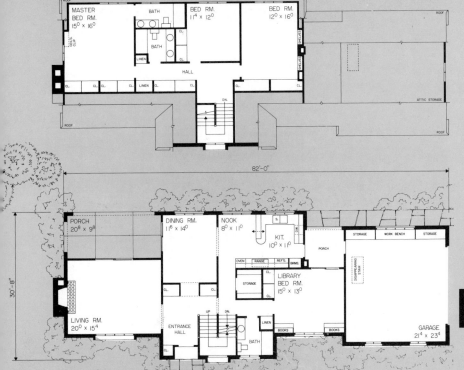

Design 122273

1,357 Sq. Ft. - First Floor
1,065 Sq. Ft. - Second Floor; 38,303 Cu. Ft.

● Note the traditional charm of this design. Formal/informal dining areas are offered in this plan. The large living room with fireplace will provide a lot of enjoyment. A full bath, storage area and your option of a library/bedroom also are featured on this floor. The second floor has a large master bedroom with a full bath. Two bedrooms and another full bath will serve the rest of the family.

Design 122278

1,804 Sq. Ft. - First Floor
939 Sq. Ft. - Second Floor
44,274 Cu. Ft.

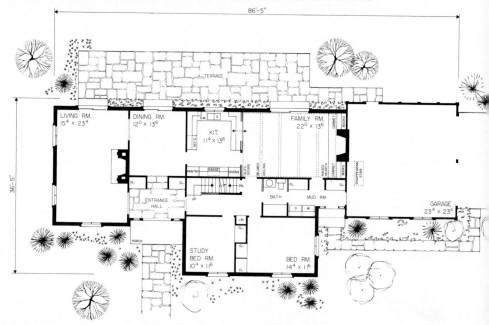

● The Tudor charm is characterized in each of these three one-and-a-half story designs. Study each of them for its own special features.

Design 122242 1,327 Sq. Ft. - First Floor
832 Sq. Ft. - Second Floor; 35,315 Cu. Ft.

● Here is a Tudor adaptation with unique appeal. The main, two-story section is flanked by two, one-story wings. The roof, projecting from the second floor, results in a covered, front porch. Beam work, stucco, diamond-lite windows and brick masses go along with good proportion to create an eye-catching exterior. This home gives the appearance of being much larger than it really is with the garage opening to the side. Inside - the spacious entrance hall routes traffic most effectively. It is flanked by the formal dining and living rooms.

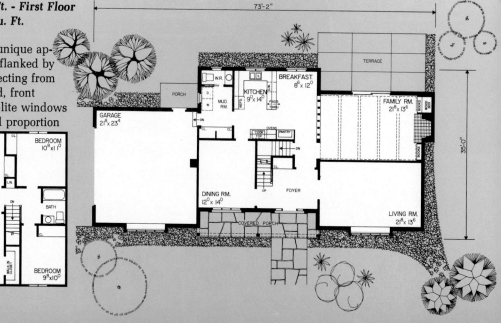

This is a most interesting home; both inside and out. Its L-shape with covered front porch and diamond-lite windows is appealing. Its floor plan with extra bedroom, lounge and storage room is exceptional.

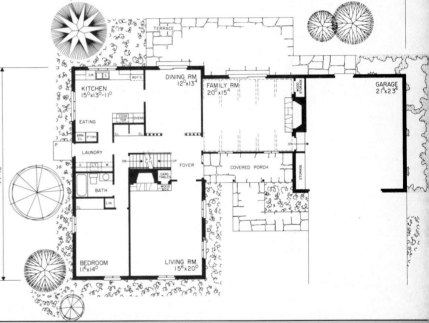

Design 122241
1,617 Sq. Ft. - First Floor
1,348 Sq. Ft. - Second Floor
43,225 Cu. Ft.

Design 122127 1,712 Sq. Ft. - First Floor
450 Sq. Ft. - Second Floor; 39,435 Cu. Ft.

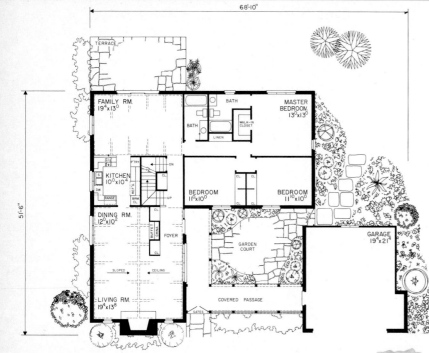

ALTERNATE MASTER SUITE

● Features of this design are plenty - both inside and out. A list of the exterior design highlights is most interesting. It begins with the character created by the impressive roof surfaces. The U-shape creates a unique appeal and results in the formation of a garden court. A covered passage provides the court with its complete privacy from the street. List your favorite interior features. Note the optional second floor master suite.

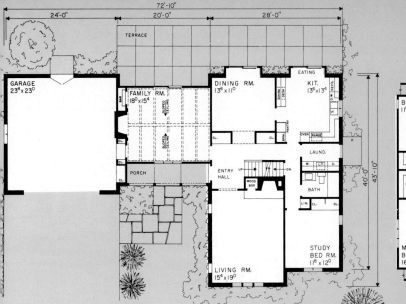

Design 122126
1,566 Sq. Ft. - First Floor
930 Sq. Ft. - Second Floor; 38,122 Cu. Ft.

● The configuration of this home is interesting. Its L-shape allows for flexible placement on your lot which makes it ideal for a corner lot. Exterior Tudor detailing is outstanding. Interior living potential is also excellent. Large formal and informal rooms are on the first floor along with the kitchen, dining room, laundry and spare bedroom or study. Three more bedrooms are on the second floor. Closets are plentiful throughout.

Design 122274 1,941 Sq. Ft. - First Floor
1,392 Sq. Ft. - Second Floor; 32,580 Cu. Ft.

● This home is a distinctive Tudor adaptation. Imagine how you and your family will enjoy outdoor living with the entrance court and the terraces. Study the location of the work center and how it relates to the dining and family rooms. There are four bedrooms - two downstairs and two up. Blueprints include optional basement.

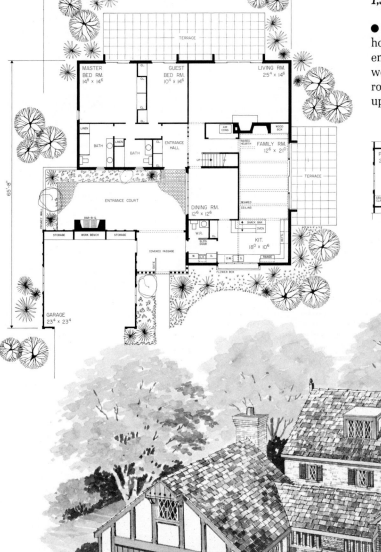

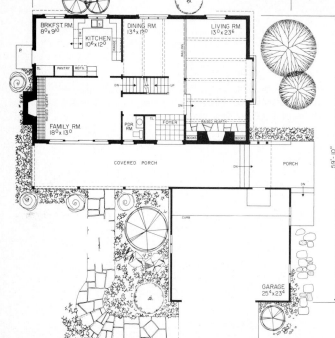

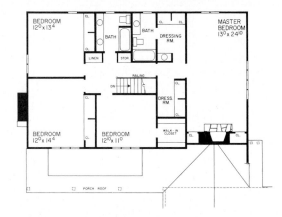

Design 122324 1,256 Sq. Ft. - First Floor
1,351 Sq. Ft. - Second Floor; 37,603 Cu. Ft.

● Dramatic, indeed! Both the interior and the exterior of these three Tudor designs deserve mention. Study each of them closely. The design featured here has a simple rectangular plan which will be relatively economical to build. This design is ideal for a corner lot.

Design 122854 1,261 Sq. Ft. - First Floor
950 Sq. Ft. - Second Floor; 36,820 Cu. Ft.

● The charm of old England has been captured in this outstanding one-and-a-half story design. Interior livability will efficiently serve the various needs of all family members. The first floor offers both formal and informal areas, along with the work centers. Features include: a wet-bar in the dining room, the kitchen's snack bar, first floor laundry and covered porch.

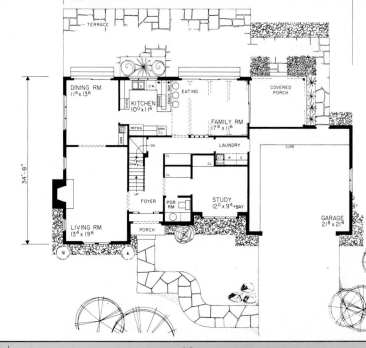

Design 122577
1,718 Sq. Ft. - First Floor
1,147 Sq. Ft. - Second Floor; 42,843 Cu. Ft.

● The exterior of this Tudor has interesting roof planes, delightful window treatment and recessed front entrance. The master suite with sitting room is one of the highlights of the interior.

Design 122674
1,922 Sq. Ft. - First Floor
890 Sq. Ft. - Second Floor; 37,411 Cu. Ft.

● This delightful Tudor design's configuration permits a flexible orientation on its site with either the garage doors or the front doors facing the street. One-and-a-half-story designs offer great flexibilty in their livability. Complete livability is offered on the first floor then by utilizing the second floor another three bedrooms and bath are available. First floor features include a sunken family room with fireplace and built-in bookshelves, rear living room with sliding glass doors to the terrace, large formal dining room, first floor laundry and two washrooms.

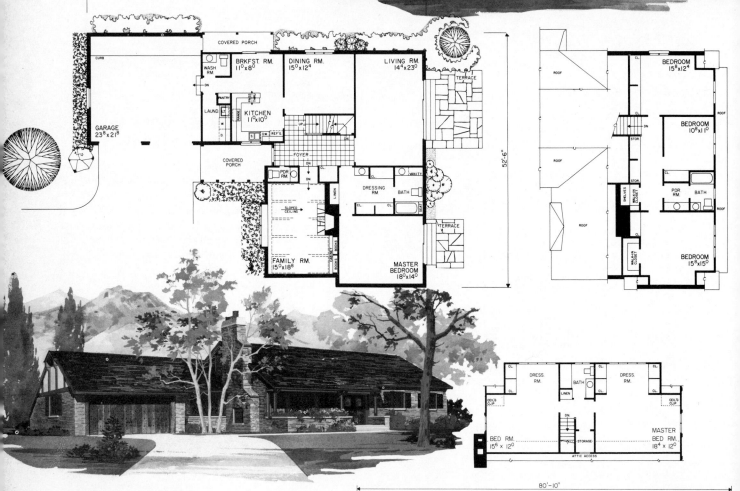

Design 122286
1,496 Sq. Ft. - First Floor
751 Sq. Ft. - Second Floor; 32,165 Cu. Ft.

● This charming home has a hint of Tudor styling. It will offer you and your family lots of livability. Take note of the spacious living room with fireplace. Just a few steps away, you can easily entertain family and friends in the sizable family-dining room. It is attractively highlighted with a beamed ceiling. Access to the rear terrace is obtained from both family room and nook area. A nice sized kitchen overlooks the terrace. Two bedrooms and a full bath also are on this floor. The development of the second floor adds two more bedrooms and another bath.

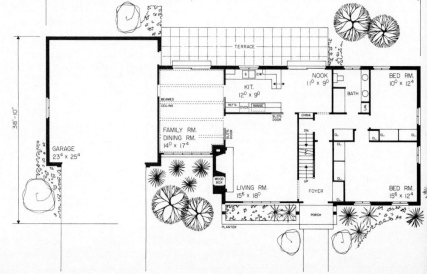

TRADITIONAL VARIATIONS . . . as featured

in this section highlight first and foremost pleasing exterior proportions. It is this characteristic that pleases the eye and holds it to further appreciate a fine design's other marks of distinction. As you review these houses note the window treatment, the doorway detailing, the roof
lines, the structure's configuration and other appointments such as cupolas, carriage lamps, dovecotes, and exterior materials. A study of the
floor plans will reveal mud rooms, first floor laundries, extra baths, formal and informal dining facilities, efficient kitchen work centers, family rooms, studies, lounges, beamed ceilings, raised hearth fireplaces, etc. Don't overlook the indoor-outdoor living relationships.

Design 122174

1,506 Sq. Ft. - First Floor
1,156 Sq. Ft. - Second Floor
37,360 Cu. Ft.

● Your building budget could
hardly buy more charm, or
greater livability. The appeal
of the exterior is wrapped up
in a myriad of design features.
They include: the interesting
roof lines; the effective use of
brick and horizontal siding; the
delightful window treatment;
the covered front porch; the
chimney and dovecote
detailing. The livability of the
interior is represented by a
long list of convenient living
features. There is a formal
area consisting of a living room
with fireplace and dining
room. The family room has a
raised hearth fireplace, wood
box and beamed ceiling. Also
on the first floor is a kitchen,
laundry and bedroom with
adjacent bath. Three bedrooms,
lounge and two baths upstairs
plus plenty of closets and bulk
storage over garage. Don't overlook the sliding glass doors,
the breakfast area and the
basement. An excellent plan.

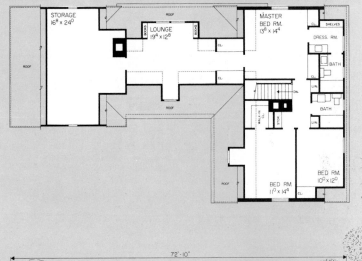

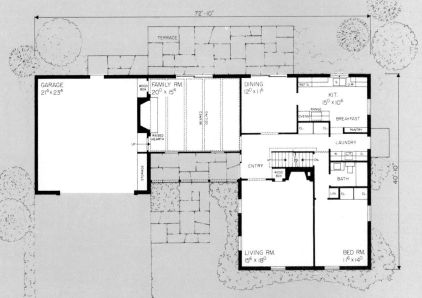

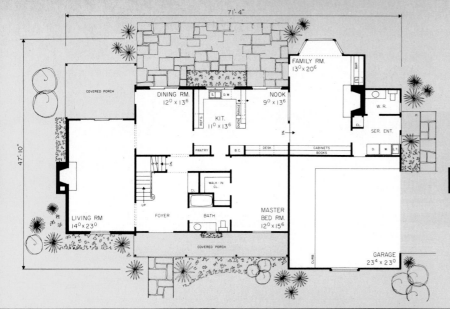

Design 122500
1,851 Sq. Ft. - First Floor
762 Sq. Ft. - Second Floor
43,052 Cu. Ft.

● The large family will enjoy the wonderful living patterns offered by this charming home. Don't miss the covered rear porch and the many features of the family room.

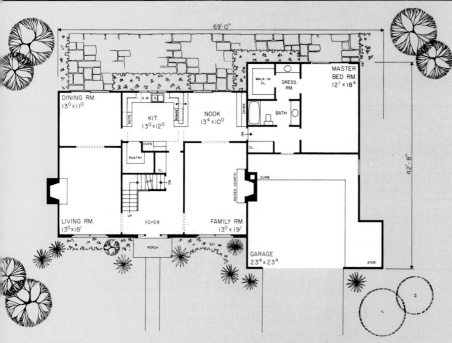

Design 122501
1,699 Sq. Ft. - First Floor
758 Sq. Ft. - Second Floor
37,693 Cu. Ft.

● Whether you build this inviting home with a fieldstone front, or substitute with a different material of your choice, you can be assured that you've selected a great home for your family.

Design 122338
1,505 Sq. Ft. - First Floor
1,219 Sq. Ft. - Second Floor
38,878 Cu. Ft.

● A spacious receiving hall is a fine setting for the welcoming of guests. Here traffic flows effectively to all areas of the plan. Outstanding livability throughout the entire plan.

● If symmetry means any-
thing, this pleasant house
has it. The projecting wings
of the sleeping zone and the
garage are virtually identical.
However, the appeal of this
charmer does not end with
its symmetrical beauty.
There is a world of livability
to be fostered by this home.

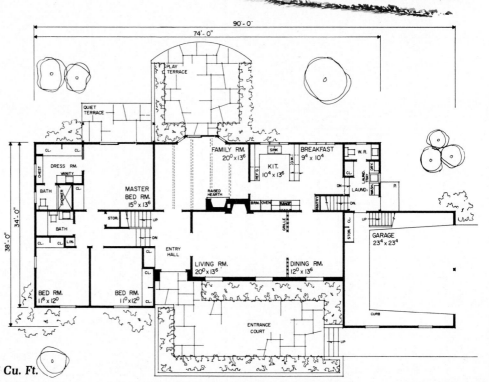

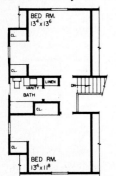

Design 121964
2,150 Sq. Ft. - First Floor
680 Sq. Ft. - Second Floor; 39,927 Cu. Ft.

Design 121780 2,018 Sq. Ft. - First Floor
568 Sq. Ft. - Second Floor; 37,586 Cu. Ft.

● Here is a U-shaped story-and-a-half
which has an abundance of livable floor
area. Imagine, here are five bedrooms and
three full baths, plus plenty of storage to
serve the large family. There will be a
choice of eating places: kitchen, dining room
or snack bar.

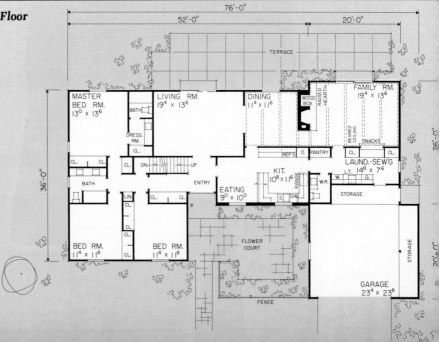

Design 121967 1,804 Sq. Ft. - First Floor
496 Sq. Ft. - Second Floor; 40,173 Cu. Ft.

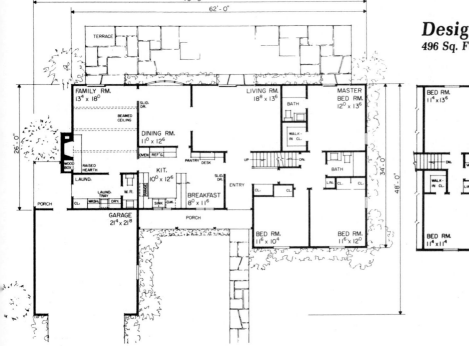

● You'll always want that first impression your guests get of your new home to be a lasting one. There will be much that will linger in the memories of most of your visitors after their visit to this home. Of course, the impressive exterior will long be remembered. And little wonder with its distinctive projecting garage and bedroom wing, its recessed front porch, its horizontal siding and its interesting roof lines. Inside, there is much to behold. The presence of five bedrooms and three full baths will not be forgotten soon. Formal and informal areas will serve every family occasion.

● A versatile plan, wrapped in a pleasing traditional facade, to cater to the demands of even the most active of families. There is plenty of living space for both formal and informal activities. With two bedrooms upstairs and two down, sleeping accommodations are excellently planned to serve all.

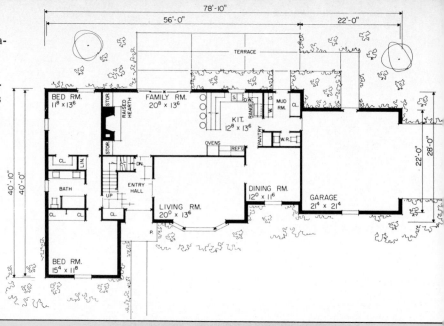

● A study of the first and second floors of this charming design will reveal that nothing has been omitted to assure convenient living. List your family's living requirements and then observe how this house will proceed to satisfy them. Features galore.

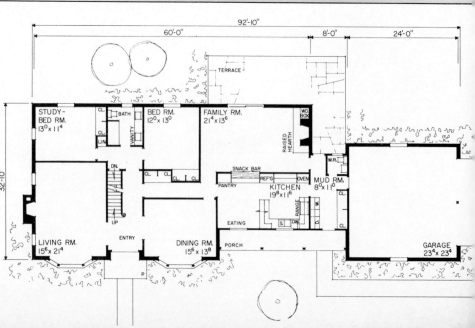

● A great plan! The large family will find its living requirements satisfied admirably all throughout those active years of growing up. This would make a fine expansible house. The upstairs may be finished off as the size of the family increases and budget permits. Complete living requirements can be obtained on the first floor.

Design 121790 1,782 Sq. Ft. - First Floor; 920 Sq. Ft. - Second Floor; 37,359 Cu. Ft.

Design 121736 1,618 Sq. Ft. - First Floor; 952 Sq. Ft. - Second Floor; 34,106 Cu. Ft.

Design 121793 1,986 Sq. Ft. - First Floor; 944 Sq. Ft. - Second Floor; 35,800 Cu. Ft.

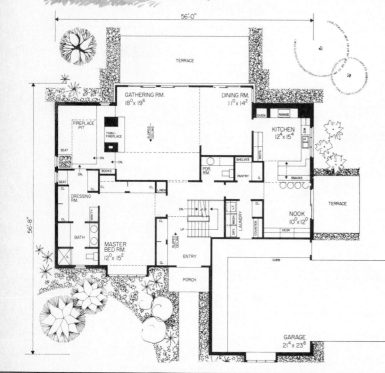

● You and your family will love the new living patterns you'll experience in this story-and-a-half home. The front entry hall features an impressive open staircase to the upstairs and basement. Adjacent is the master bedroom which has a compartmented bath with both tub and stall shower. The spacious dressing room steps down into a unique, sunken conversation pit. This cozy area has a planter, built-in seat and a view of the thru-fireplace, opening to the gathering room as well. Here, the ceiling slopes to the top of the second floor lounge which looks down into the gathering room.

Design 122718 1,941 Sq. Ft. - First Floor
791 Sq. Ft. - Second Floor; 49,895 Cu. Ft.

Design 122513
1,799 Sq. Ft. - First Floor
1,160 Sq. Ft. - Second Floor
47,461 Cu. Ft.

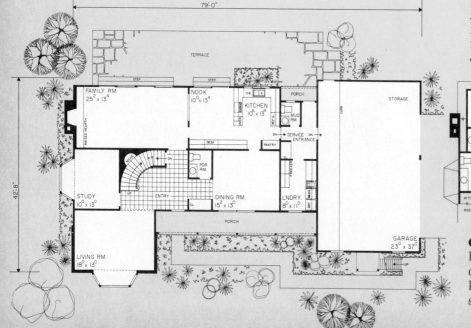

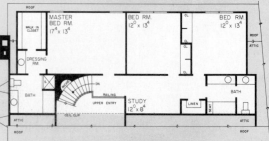

● What an appealing story-and-a-half design. Delightful, indeed, is the colonial detailing of the garage. The large entry hall with its open curving staircase is dramatic.

TERRACE   TERRACE

FAMILY RM.
13⁸ x 20⁰

NOOK
8⁰ x 13⁰

KITCHEN
10⁰ x 13⁶

DINING RM.
13⁰ x 13⁶

DESK   OVEN   P'TRY.

HALL   DN.   REF'G.

LAUNDRY

DRY WASH

WASH RM.   BOOKS   CAB'T.

STOR. B.C.

SEAT   CL.   PORCH

SERVICE ENTRANCE

STUDY
15⁸ x 11⁶

ENTRY   UP

PORCH

LIVING RM.
15⁸ x 27⁴

CURB

GARAGE
25⁴ x 23⁴

66'-8"

62'-8"

Design 122757
2,052 Sq. Ft. - First Floor
1,425 Sq. Ft. - Second Floor; 56,775 Cu. Ft.

● An L-shaped story-and-a-half with a traditional facade is hard to beat for pure charm. Here, the use of contrasting exterior materials - fieldstone, brick, vertical siding - along with delightful window treatment, recessed front door, carriage lamps, two massive chimneys and a cupola all make a contribution to outright appeal.

ROOF   ROOF

MASTER BED RM.
13⁰ x 20⁴

BED RM.
11⁴ x 11²

LOUNGE/BED RM.
13⁰ x 13⁶

BED RM.
9⁰-16⁰ x 20⁸

BATH

DRESSING ROOM

LINEN   CL.   CL.

WALK-IN CLOSET

CL.   TUB   BATH

DN.

SITTING RM.
9⁰ x 5⁰

ATTIC

Design 121242 1,872 Sq. Ft. - First Floor
982 Sq. Ft. - Second Floor; 29,221 Cu. Ft.

● Here are three long, low one-and-a-half story designs with all the traditional charm one would wish for a new home. The floor plans offer all the livability an active family would want. Which is your favorite design?

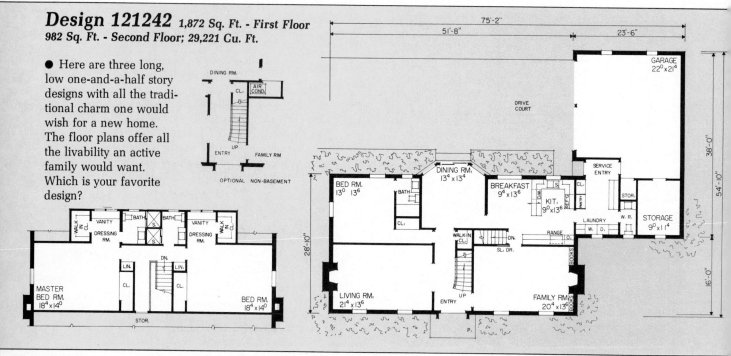

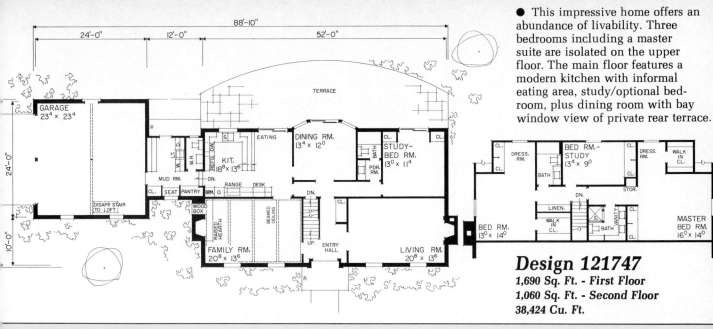

● This impressive home offers an abundance of livability. Three bedrooms including a master suite are isolated on the upper floor. The main floor features a modern kitchen with informal eating area, study/optional bedroom, plus dining room with bay window view of private rear terrace.

Design 121747
1,690 Sq. Ft. - First Floor
1,060 Sq. Ft. - Second Floor
38,424 Cu. Ft.

Design 121906 1,514 Sq. Ft. - First Floor
992 Sq. Ft. - Second Floor; 37,311 Cu. Ft.

● This charming, one-and-a-half story home definitely extends an invitation of warmth in appearance. Once inside this home, you will be surprised at its many fine features. Study the floor plan and list your favorite features.

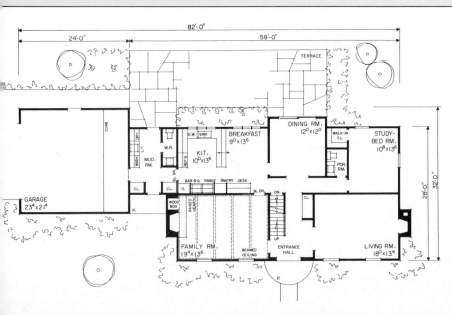

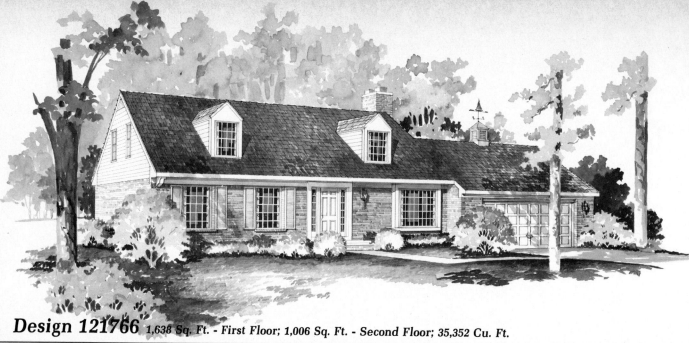

Design 121766 *1,638 Sq. Ft. - First Floor; 1,006 Sq. Ft. - Second Floor; 35,352 Cu. Ft.*

● Here is a home that truly fits the description of traditional charm. The symmetry is, indeed, delightful. A certain magnetic aura seems to reach out with a whisper of welcome. Observe the spacious family-kitchen area, the study, the separate dining room and the extra bath.

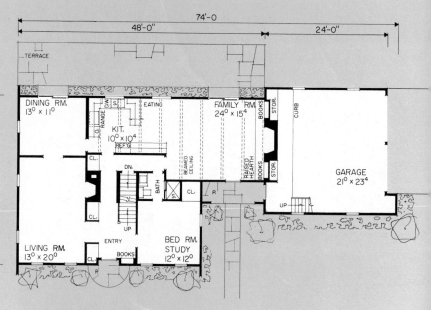

Design 122124
1,180 Sq. Ft. - First Floor
1,018 Sq. Ft. - Second Floor; 29,854 Cu. Ft.

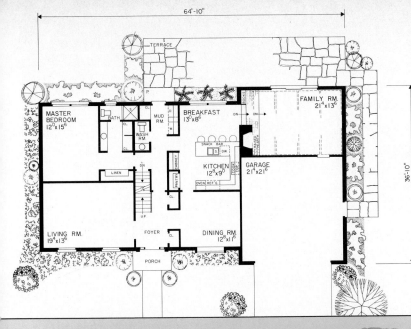

● This cozy home has over 2,600 square feet of livable floor area! And the manner in which this space is put to work to function conveniently for the large family is worth studying. Imagine five bedrooms, three full baths, living, dining and family rooms. Note large kitchen.

Design 121701 1,344 Sq. Ft. - First Floor; 948 Sq. Ft. - Second Floor; 33,952 Cu. Ft.

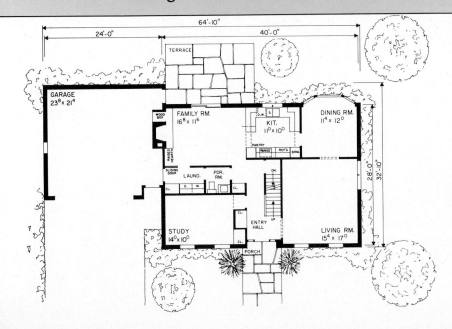

● Here is a home that truly fits the description of traditional charm. The symmetry is, indeed, delightful. A certain magnetic aura seems to reach out with a whisper of welcome. Observe the spacious family-kitchen area, the study, the separate dining room and the extra bath.

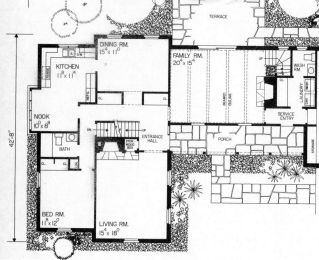

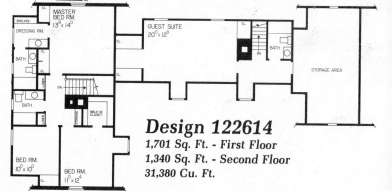

● Pleasing appearance! With an excellent floor plan. Notice how all the rooms are accessible from a hall. That's a plus for easy housekeeping. Some other extras: an exceptionally large family room which is more than 20' x 15', a gracious living room, formal dining room adjacent to the kitchen/nook area, four large bedrooms, a secluded guest suite plus a huge storage area.

Note that the large guest suite, featuring a full bath, is only accessible by the back stairs in the family room. You could use it as a spacious library, playroom or a hobby area. Two fireplaces (one with a built-in wood box), walk-in closets, covered front porch and rear terrace also highlight this home.

Design 122614
1,701 Sq. Ft. - First Floor
1,340 Sq. Ft. - Second Floor
31,380 Cu. Ft.

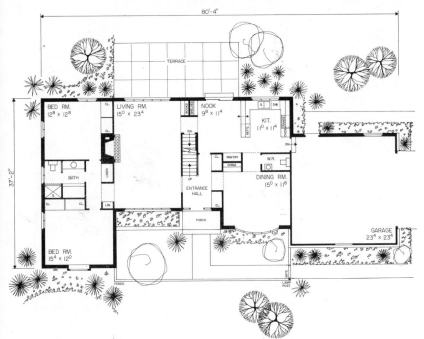

Design 122284
1,677 Sq. Ft. - First Floor
897 Sq. Ft. - Second Floor; 40,413 Cu. Ft.

● This low-slung traditional design features four bedrooms, two up and two down, plus three baths and a washroom. The spacious living room will efficiently serve all of the family activities. There is a basement for family recreational and hobby space.

Design 122285
1,118 Sq. Ft. - First Floor
821 Sq. Ft. - Second Floor
28,585 Cu. Ft.

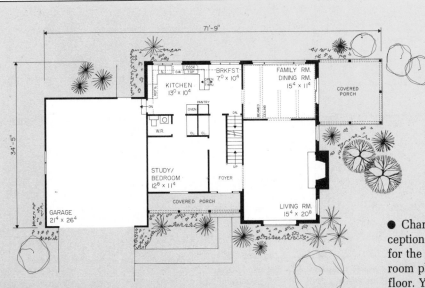

● Charm is found in this appealing home. There is exceptional livability in this one-and-a-half story design for the average sized family. Note the flexibility in the room planning. Rooms have optional usage on the first floor. You decide how your family will live.

● It will certainly be fun living in this traditional home. You'll have many options as to how you may use some of the rooms.

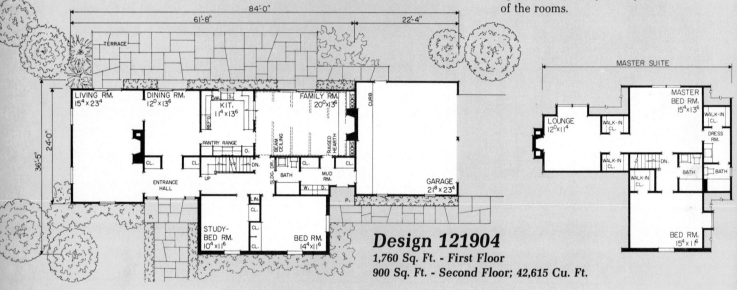

84'-0"

61'-8"   22'-4"

TERRACE

36'-5"   24'-0"

LIVING RM. 15⁴ x 23⁴

DINING RM. 12⁰ x 13⁶

KIT. 11⁴ x 13⁶

FAMILY RM. 20⁰ x 13⁶

CURB

PANTRY RANGE

BEAM CEILING

RAISED HEARTH

ENTRANCE HALL

BATH

MUD RM.

GARAGE 21⁸ x 23⁴

STUDY-BED RM. 10⁴ x 11⁶

BED RM. 14⁴ x 11⁶

MASTER SUITE

LOUNGE 12⁰ x 11⁴

WALK-IN CL.

MASTER BED RM. 15⁴ x 13⁶

WALK-IN CL.

DRESS RM.

WALK-IN CL.

WALK-IN CL.

BATH

BATH

BED RM. 15⁴ x 1⁶

Design 121904
1,760 Sq. Ft. - First Floor
900 Sq. Ft. - Second Floor; 42,615 Cu. Ft.

Design 121794 2,122 Sq. Ft. - First Floor
802 Sq. Ft. - Second Floor; 37,931 Cu. Ft.

● The inviting warmth of this delightful home tickles the eye of even the most casual planner. Imagine, four big bedrooms! Formal and informal living can be enjoyed throughout this charming plan. A private, formal dining room is available for those very special occasions.

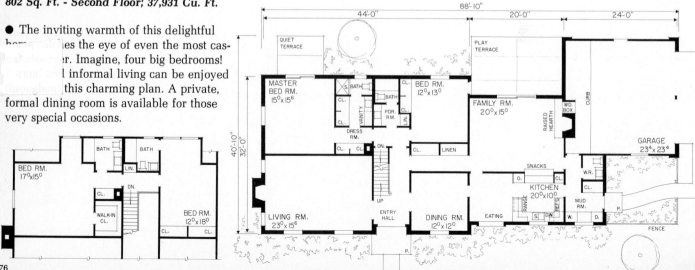

88'-10"

44'-0"   20'-0"   24'-0"

QUIET TERRACE

PLAY TERRACE

40'-10"   32'-0"

MASTER BED RM. 15⁰ x 15⁶

BATH

BED RM. 12⁰ x 13⁰

FAMILY RM. 20⁰ x 15⁰

WD. BOX

CURB

DRESS RM.

VANITY

PDR. RM.

LIN.

LINEN

RAISED HEARTH

GARAGE 23⁴ x 23⁴

LIVING RM. 23⁰ x 15⁶

ENTRY HALL

DINING RM. 12⁰ x 12⁰

EATING

SNACKS

KITCHEN 20⁰ x 10⁰

RANGE

REFG.

MUD RM.

W.R.

FENCE

UP

BED RM. 17⁰ x 15⁰

BATH

BATH

LIN.

DN.

WALK-IN CL.

BED RM. 12⁰ x 18⁰

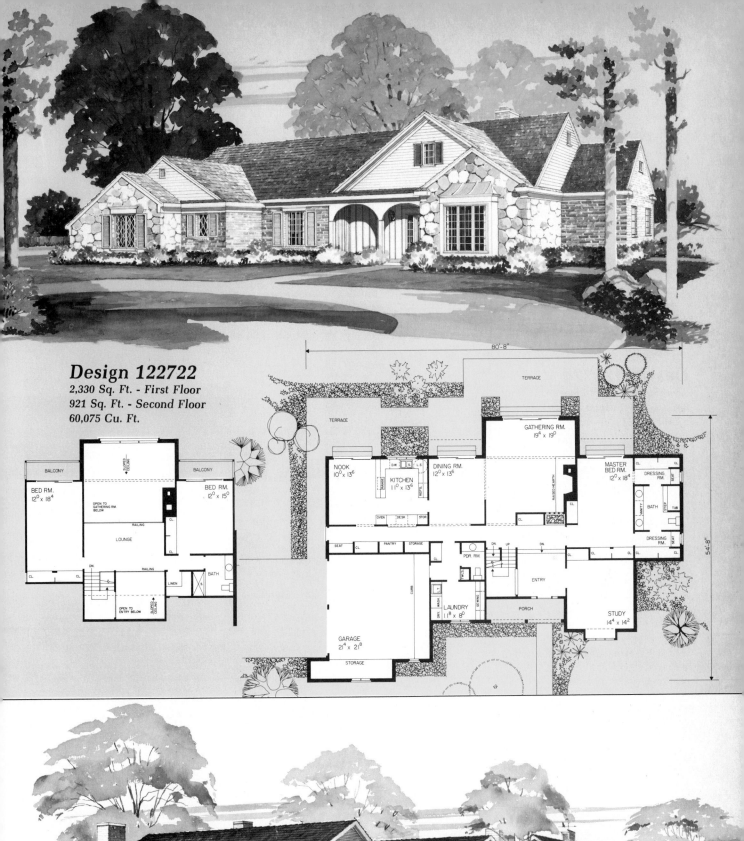

Design 122722
2,330 Sq. Ft. - First Floor
921 Sq. Ft. - Second Floor
60,075 Cu. Ft.

Second Floor:

BALCONY

SLOPED CEILING

BALCONY

BED RM.
12^0 x 18^4

OPEN TO GATHERING RM. BELOW

RAILING

BED RM.
12^0 x 15^0

LOUNGE

CL

DN.

RAILING

CL

BATH

LINEN

OPEN TO ENTRY BELOW

SLOPED CEILING

First Floor:

80'-8"

TERRACE

TERRACE

GATHERING RM.
19^4 x 19^0

NOOK
10^0 x 13^6

DINING RM.
12^0 x 13^6

KITCHEN
11^0 x 13^6

RANGE

D.W.

REFG.

RAISED HEARTH

CL

MASTER BED RM.
12^0 x 18^4

DRESSING RM.

SEAT

VANITY

BATH

STEP

TUB

OVEN

DESK

STOR.

CL

DRESSING RM.

SEAT

SEAT

CL

PANTRY

STORAGE

PDR. RM.

DN.

UP

DN.

ENTRY

CL

CL

CL

54'-8"

CURB

WASH

LAUNDRY
11^8 x 8^0

DRY.

PORCH

STUDY
14^4 x 14^2

GARAGE
21^4 x 21^8

STORAGE

Design 122724

2,543 Sq. Ft. - First Floor
884 Sq. Ft. - Second Floor
53,640 Cu. Ft.

● Impressive at first glance! The interior of this one-and-a-half story home offers an abundance of livability. The master bedroom suite is on the first floor and has a private terrace. The second floor houses two more bedrooms and a bath. A design sure to provide enjoyment.

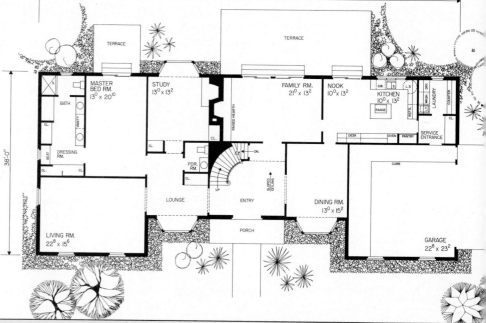

Design 122676
1,889 Sq. Ft. - First Floor
872 Sq. Ft. - Second Floor; 39,003 Cu. Ft.

● Here is the perfect home for those who want lots of livability. Note the easy access to each room. A luxurious master bedroom suite will provide all of the comforts you deserve. Take note of the sitting room, his/her dressing and closet areas and the raised tub. Upstairs, two nice sized bedrooms and a full bath.

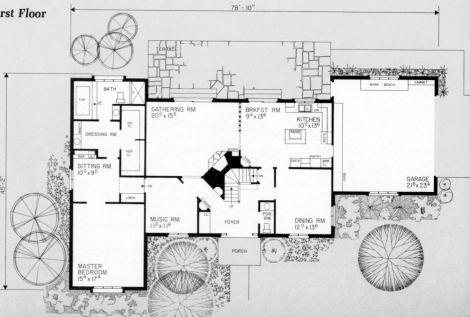

Design 122313 1,446 Sq. Ft. - First Floor
985 Sq. Ft. - Second Floor; 33,544 Cu. Ft.

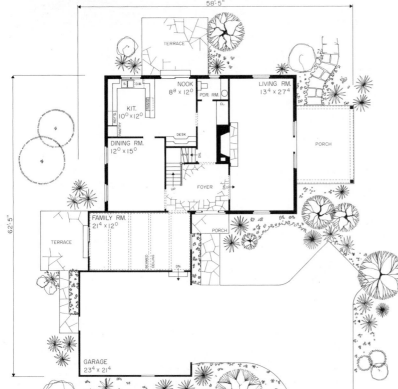

● This charming, one-and-a-half story house will embrace you with its cozy appeal. A spacious living room is to the right after entering this home. It has a fireplace that is sure to bring many hours of pleasure in the cold winter months. Note its easy access to the covered porch. Left of the foyer, you will find a good sized family room with beamed ceiling and a formal dining room. Nearby is an efficient kitchen and adjacent nook. Note the built-in desk. Upstairs, a master bedroom, two smaller bedrooms and a bath will serve the family. Because of its configuration, this design is ideal for a corner lot.

Design 121115 1,440 Sq. Ft. - First Floor
740 Sq. Ft. - Second Floor; 33,516 Cu. Ft.

● A most distinctive exterior with an equally distinctive interior. A study of the plan reveals all of the elements to assure convenient living. The main living unit, the first floor, functions very efficiently. Two bedrooms and a full bath comprise the sleeping zone. The U-shaped kitchen is very efficient. The family/dining room will serve the family admirably. Adjacent to the kitchen is the laundry area, washroom and entrance from the garage. This living unit is definitely complete. Now add the second floor. Absolutely fantastic! The whole second floor is a master bedroom.

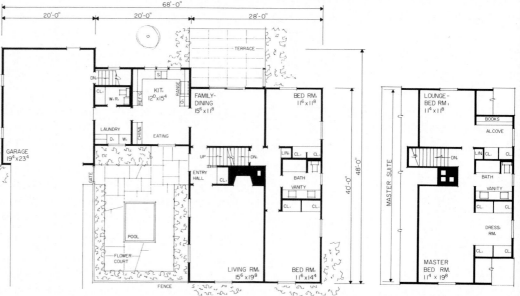

Design 121196 1,008 Sq. Ft. - First Floor
648 Sq. Ft. - Second Floor; 23,884 Cu. Ft.

● This cozy home is ideal for a small family. Upon entering this house, you will find a nice sized living room with a fireplace. Adjacent, the formal dining area has sliding glass doors leading to the terrace. The kitchen and informal eating area are just a few steps away. A full bath and an optional bedroom/study also are on this floor. A full bath and two good sized bedrooms, each with its own dressing area, are on the second floor.

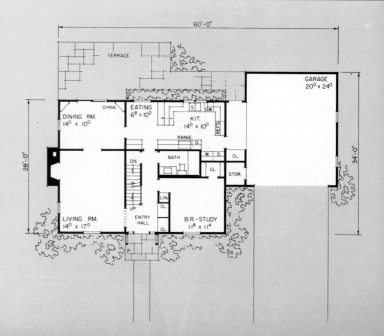

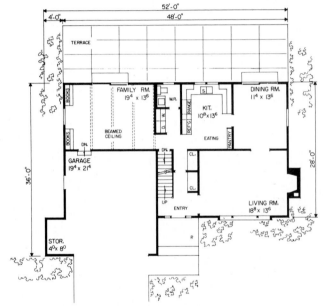

Design 121241 1,064 Sq. Ft. - First Floor
898 Sq. Ft. - Second Floor; 24,723 Cu. Ft.

● You don't need a mansion to live graciously. What you do need is a practical floor plan which takes into consideration the varied activities of the busy family. This plan does that! This story-and-a-half design will not require a large piece of property while it returns the maximum per construction dollar. Its living potential is tremendous.

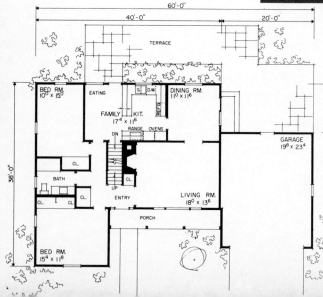

Design 123131 1,166 Sq. Ft. - First Floor
709 Sq. Ft. - Second Floor; 29,328 Cu. Ft.

● A charming adaptation with an extra measure of exterior appeal and an outstanding array of interior features. Contributing to the beauty of the exterior is the prudent use of varying material. The covered porch, sheltering the front door, and the large living room window are highlights. Inside, there is a fine functioning floor plan. There are four bedrooms, two full baths, both a formal and an informal dining area, an excellent kitchen, a spacious living room, plenty of closets and a basement. This design could function as a three bedroom home. The breakfast room and rear bedroom could combine to make a family room.

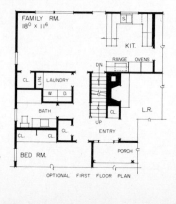

Design 121340
1,232 Sq. Ft. - First Floor
890 Sq. Ft. - Second Floor
27,796 Cu. Ft.

● The covered, front porch with its appealing columns shelters the colonial entrance of this design. The projections of the first floor bedroom wing and the two-car garage add interest to the facade. When entertaining in the living room, your guests will be but a few short steps from the separate dining room. A pass-thru permits the work center and the informal eating area to function together. Note optional first floor plan.

COUNTRY ESTATE HOUSES ... *offer to those*

with unrestricted building budgets, and a sizable building site, an opportunity to enjoy unbounded livability. Each of these impressive designs has a facade which seems to herald an interior which will cater to all the whims and wishes of the active family. Among the facilities which contribute to such gratification are the master bedroom suites, libraries, large formal and informal living areas, breakfast rooms, separate dining rooms, covered porches, sweeping terraces, excellent storage facilities, efficient kitchen work centers, dramatic fireplaces, etc.

Design 122615 2,563 Sq. Ft. - First Floor
552 Sq. Ft. - Second Floor; 59,513 Cu. Ft.

● The exterior detailing of this design recalls 18th-Century New England architecture. Enter by way of the centered front door and you are greeted into the foyer. Directly to the right is the study or optional bedroom or to the left is the living room. This large formal room features sliding glass doors to the sun-drenched solarium. The beauty of the solarium will be appreciated from the master bedroom and the dining room along with the living room.

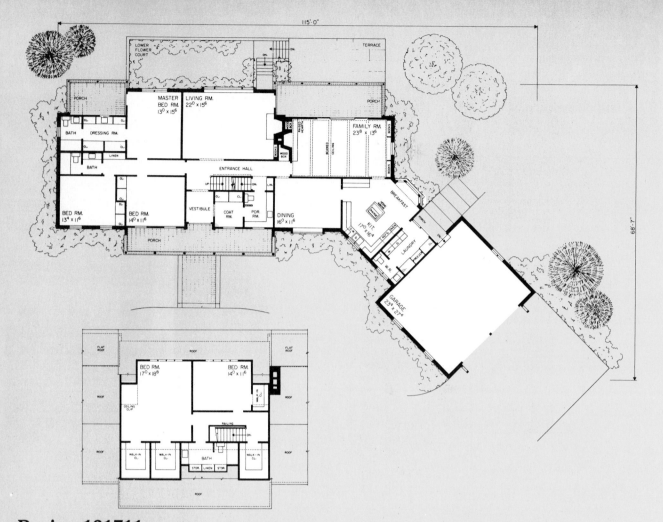

Design 121711 2,580 Sq. Ft. - First Floor; 938 Sq. Ft. - Second Floor; 46,788 Cu. Ft.

● If the gracious charm of the Colonial South appeals to you, this may be just the house you've been waiting for. There is something solid and dependable in its well-balanced facade and wide, pillared front porch. Much of the interest generated by this design comes from its interesting expanses of roof and angular projection of its kitchen and garage. The feeling of elegance is further experienced upon stepping inside, through double doors, to the spacious entrance hall where there is the separate coat room. Adjacent to this is the powder room, also convenient to the living areas. The work area of the kitchen and laundry room is truly outstanding. Designed as a five bedroom house, each is large. Storage and bath facilities are excellent.

Design 121787
2,656 Sq. Ft. - First Floor
744 Sq. Ft. - Second Floor
51,164 Cu. Ft.

● Can't you picture this dramatic home sitting on your property? The curving front drive is impressive as it passes the walks to the front door and the service entrance. The roof masses, the centered masonry chimney, the window symmetry and the 108 foot expanse across the front are among the features that make this a distinctive home. Of interest are the living and family rooms — both similar in size and each having its own fireplace.

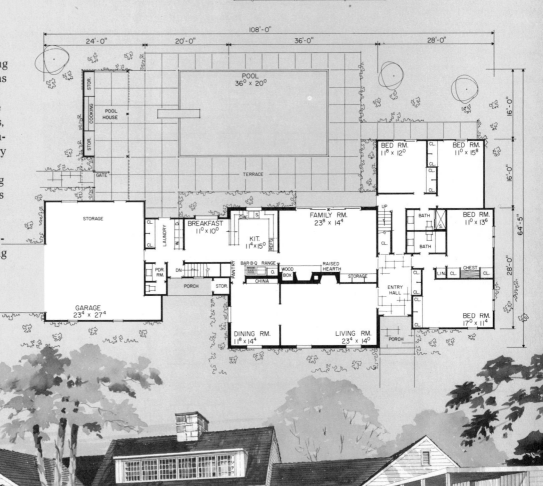

Design 122133 *3,024 Sq. Ft. - First Floor; 826 Sq. Ft. - Second Floor; 54,883 Cu. Ft.*

● A country-estate home which will command all the attention it truly deserves. The projecting pediment gable supported by the finely proportioned columns lends an aura of elegance. The window treatment, the front door detailing, the massive, capped chimney, the cupola, the brick veneer exterior and the varying roof planes complete the characterization of an impressive home. Inside, there are 3,024 square feet on the first floor. In addition, there is a two bedroom second floor should its development be necessary. However, whether called upon to function as one, or 1-1/2 story home it will provide a lifetime of gracious living. Don't overlook the compartment baths, the big library, the coat room, the beamed ceiling family room, the two fireplaces, the breakfast room and the efficient kitchen. Note pass-thru to breakfast room.

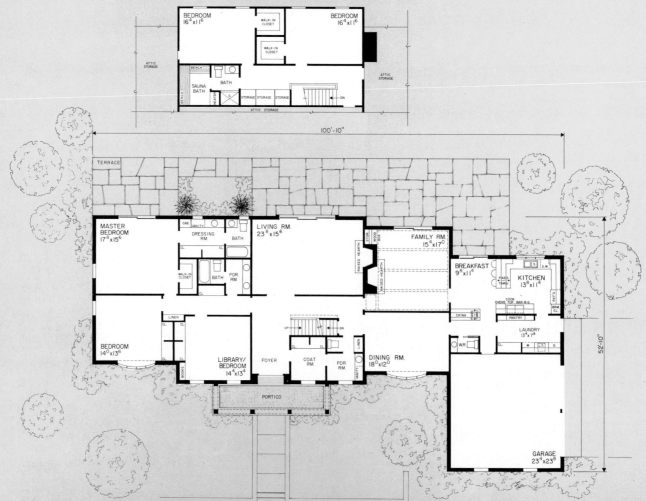

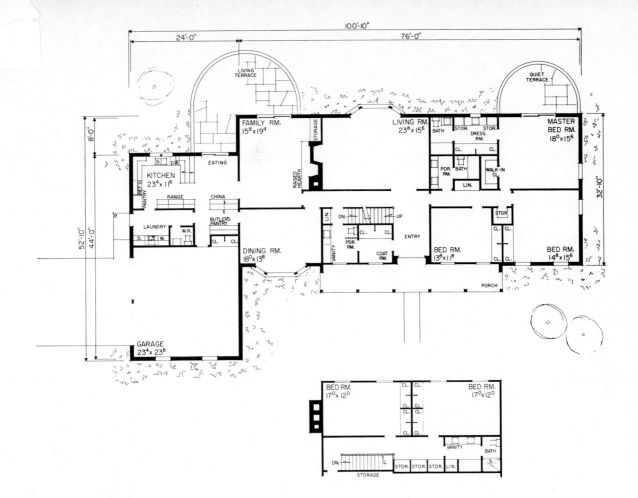

Design 121796

3,006 Sq. Ft. - First Floor
794 Sq. Ft. - Second Floor; 44,240 Cu. Ft.

● Five big bedrooms! Or make it three if you prefer not to develop the second floor. When viewing this home the initial lingering look turns into something of a studied analysis; for here is a positively outstanding design. The columned porch creates an at-

mosphere of charming country-estate living. Note that there is a living terrace plus a quiet terrace off the master bedroom. The floor plan will surely permit the fulfillment of such a way of life. Each and every member of the family will love the spaciousness of

the interior. In addition to such big and obvious features as the delightful living, dining and family rooms, the fireplaces, kitchen and three baths, there is a multitude of little features. Be sure to list them, you'll find them most interesting.

Design 121228
2,583 Sq. Ft. - First Floor
697 Sq. Ft. - Second Floor
51,429 Cu. Ft.

● This beautiful house has a wealth of detail taken from the rich traditions of French Regency design. A close examination of the plan shows the careful arrangement of space for privacy as well as good circulation of traffic.

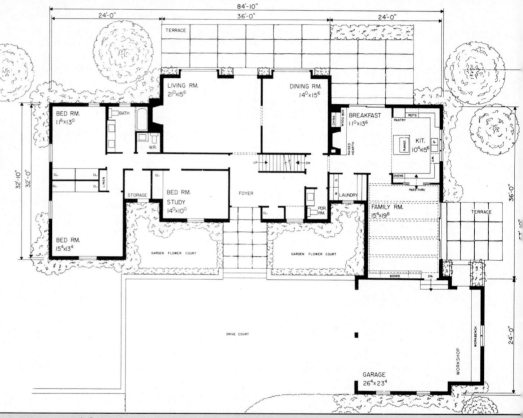

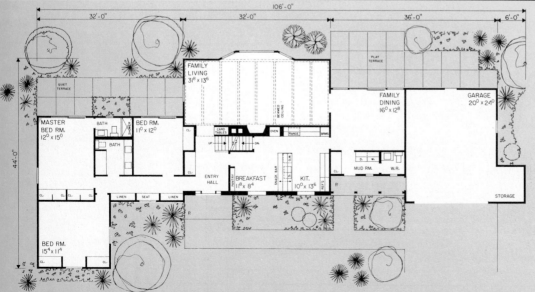

Design 121106
1,997 Sq. Ft. - First Floor
498 Sq. Ft. - Second Floor
37,678 Cu. Ft.

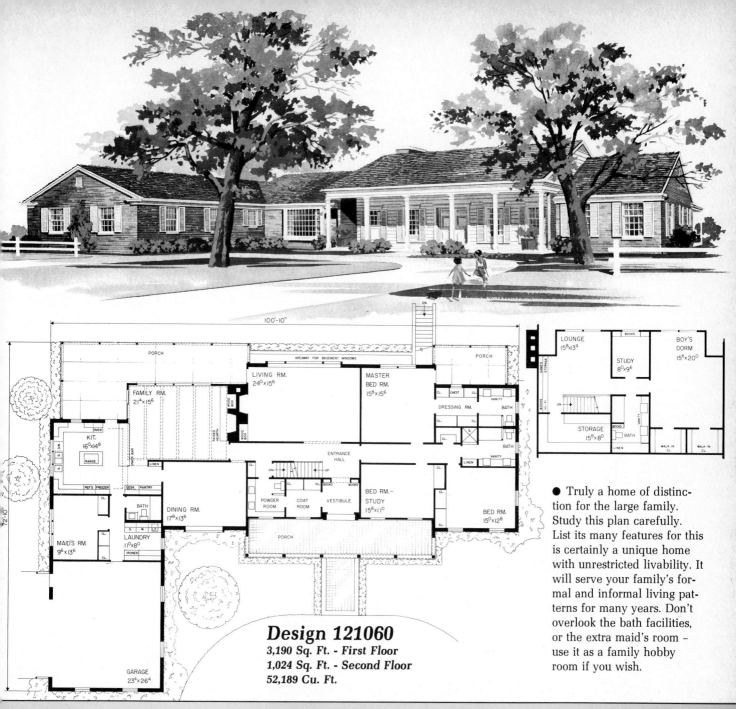

Design 121060
3,190 Sq. Ft. - First Floor
1,024 Sq. Ft. - Second Floor
52,189 Cu. Ft.

● Truly a home of distinction for the large family. Study this plan carefully. List its many features for this is certainly a unique home with unrestricted livability. It will serve your family's formal and informal living patterns for many years. Don't overlook the bath facilities, or the extra maid's room – use it as a family hobby room if you wish.

Floor plan labels:

First Floor:
- 100'-10"
- 72'-10"
- PORCH
- LIVING RM. 24⁰x15⁶
- MASTER BED RM. 15⁸x15⁶
- PORCH
- AREAWAY FOR BASEMENT WINDOWS
- FAMILY RM. 21⁴x15⁶
- DRESSING RM.
- CHEST CL CL
- VANITY
- BATH
- KIT. 16⁰x14⁸
- OVEN
- RANGE
- WOOD BOX
- RAISED HEARTH
- SNACK BAR
- LINEN
- ENTRANCE HALL
- BATH
- REF'S FREEZER
- DESK PANTRY
- CL
- DN UP
- BOOKS
- LINEN
- VANITY
- POWDER ROOM
- COAT ROOM
- VESTIBULE
- BED RM.- STUDY 15⁸x11⁰
- BED RM. 15⁰x12⁸
- CL
- MAID'S RM. 9⁶x13⁶
- BATH
- DINING RM. 17⁸x13⁶
- LAUNDRY 11⁰x8⁰
- D. W.
- IRONER
- PORCH
- GARAGE 23⁴x26⁴
- DN

Second Floor:
- LOUNGE 15⁸x13⁴
- BOOKS
- BOY'S DORM 15⁸x20⁰
- STUDY 8⁰x9⁶
- GAMES STORAGE
- BOOKS HI FI
- DN
- STORAGE 15⁸x8⁰
- VANITY
- BATH
- BOOKS
- LINEN
- WALK-IN CL.
- WALK-IN CL.

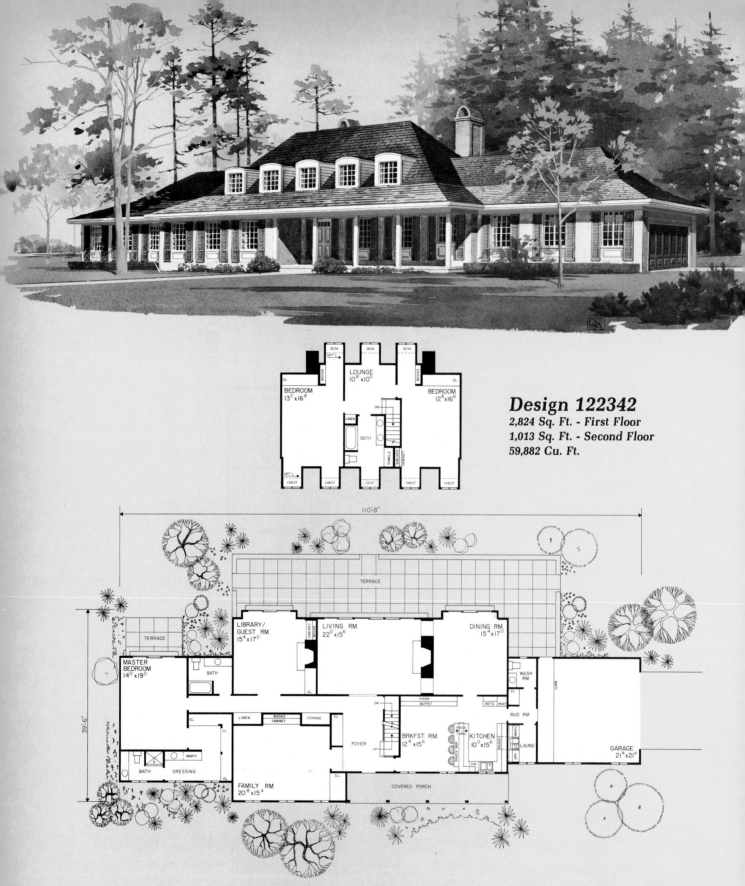

Design 122342

2,824 Sq. Ft. - First Floor
1,013 Sq. Ft. - Second Floor
59,882 Cu. Ft.

● A distinctive exterior characterized by varying roof planes, appealing window treatment, attractive chimneys and a covered front porch with prominent vertical columns. The main portion of the house is effectively balanced by the master bedroom wing on the one side and the garage wing on the other. As a buffer between house and garage is the mud room and the laundry. The kitchen is U-shaped, efficient and strategically located to serve the breakfast and dining rooms. Notice how the rooms at the rear function through sliding glass doors with the outdoor terrace areas. Fireplaces highlight both the spacious living room and the large library. The big family room features a built-in bookshelf and cabinet. Upstairs, two bedrooms and a study alcove will be found.

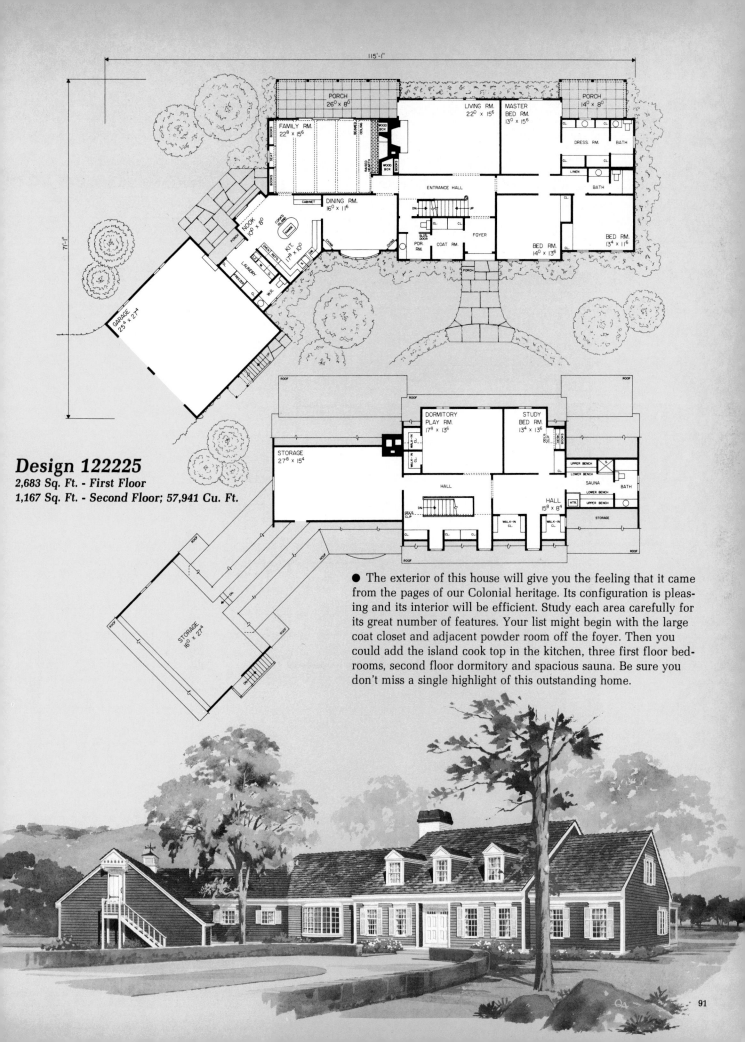

Design 122225

2,683 Sq. Ft. - First Floor
1,167 Sq. Ft. - Second Floor; 57,941 Cu. Ft.

● The exterior of this house will give you the feeling that it came from the pages of our Colonial heritage. Its configuration is pleasing and its interior will be efficient. Study each area carefully for its great number of features. Your list might begin with the large coat closet and adjacent powder room off the foyer. Then you could add the island cook top in the kitchen, three first floor bedrooms, second floor dormitory and spacious sauna. Be sure you don't miss a single highlight of this outstanding home.

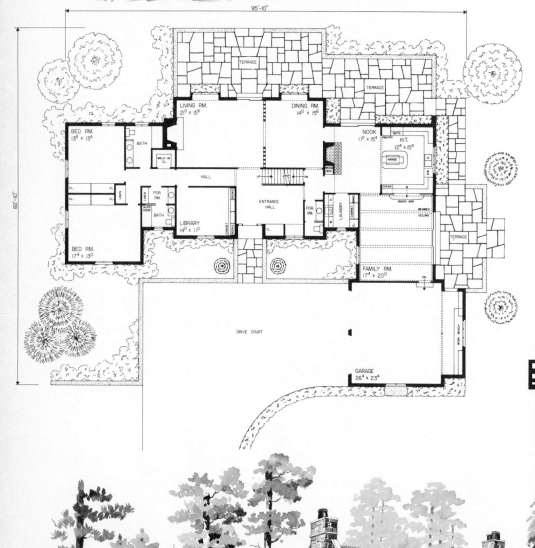

Design 122245

2,855 Sq. Ft. - First Floor
955 Sq. Ft. - Second Floor
57,645 Cu. Ft.

● The graciousness of this impressive English country house will endure for generations. The fine proportions, the exquisite architectural detailing and the interesting configuration are among the elements that create such an overwhelming measure of true character. The interior of this home will be as dramatic as the exterior. The recessed front entrance opens into a spacious, formal entrance hall. From here traffic patterns flow efficiently to all areas of the house. The garden view shows the three spacious outdoor terrace areas.

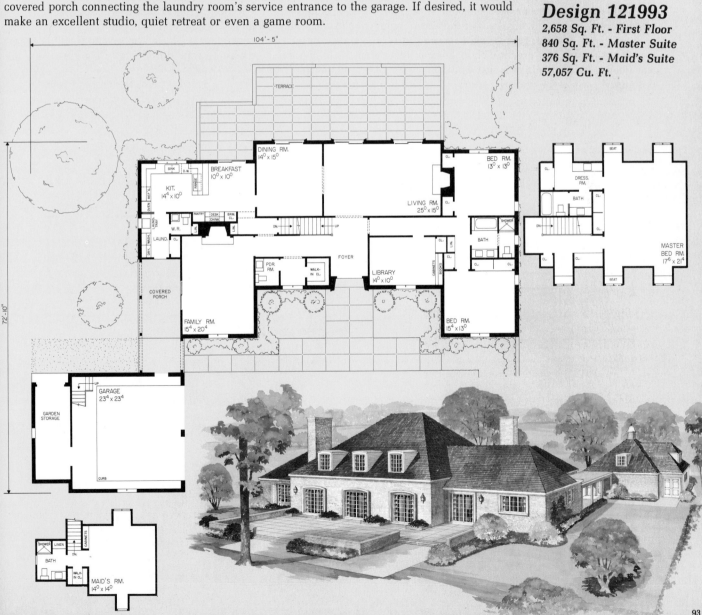

● The elegance of pleasing proportion and delightful detailing has seldom been better exemplified than by this classic French country manor adaptation. Approaching the house across the drive court, the majesty of this multi-roofed structure is breathtaking, indeed. An outstanding feature is the maid's suite. It is located above the garage and is easily reached by use of the covered porch connecting the laundry room's service entrance to the garage. If desired, it would make an excellent studio, quiet retreat or even a game room.

Design 121993
2,658 Sq. Ft. - First Floor
840 Sq. Ft. - Master Suite
376 Sq. Ft. - Maid's Suite
57,057 Cu. Ft.

● Organized zoning by room functions makes this Traditional design a comfortable home for living, as well as classic in its styling. A central foyer facilitates flexible traffic patterns. Quiet areas of the house include a media room and luxurious master bedroom suite with fitness area, spacious closet space and bath, as well as a lounge or writing area. Informal living areas of the house include a sun room, large country kitchen, and efficient kitchen with an island. Service areas include a room just off the garage for laundry, sewing, or hobbies. The second floor garage can double as a practical shop. Formal living areas include a living area and formal dining room. The second floor holds two bedrooms that would make a wonderful children's suite, with a study or TV area also upstairs.

Design 122921

3,215 Sq. Ft. - First Floor
296 Sq. Ft. - Sun Room
711 Sq. Ft. - Second Floor
69,991 Cu. Ft.

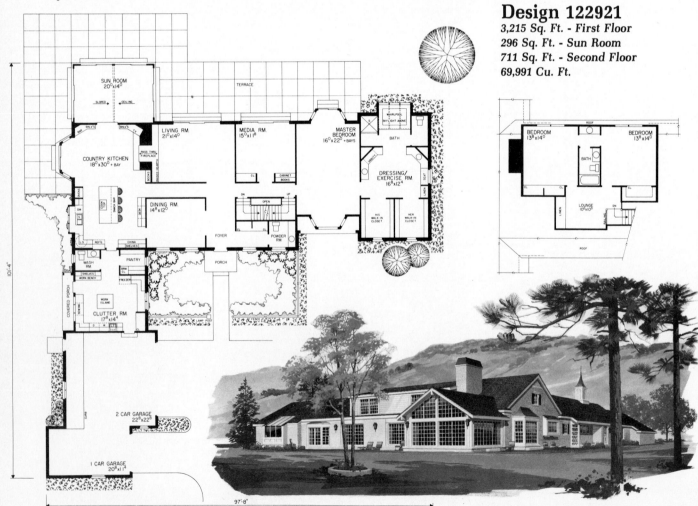

CONTEMPORARY DESIGN . . . .

has its own full measure of distinction. It is refreshing and offers clean, unfettered lines. Its forms are often unique and exciting. A review of this group of designs will reveal a wide range of differing exteriors. Each reflects its own approach to locating the sleeping area above the main floor without projecting the image of the so readily identifiable full two-story house. Therefore, note the interesting, low profiled roof lines. Because of the many interesting shapes of these contemporary houses, their plans offer unusual, yet practical and efficient, living patterns. These are sure to result in delightfully new dimensions in living.

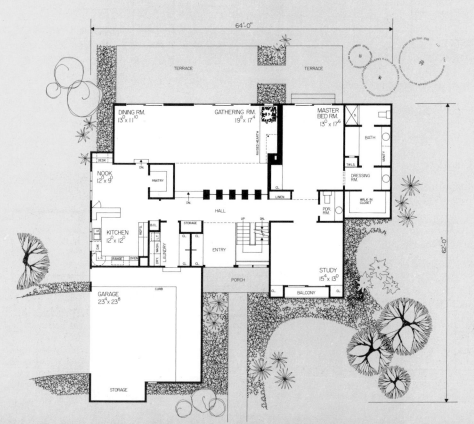

Design 122708

2,108 Sq. Ft. - First Floor
824 Sq. Ft. - Second Floor
52,170 Cu. Ft.

● Here is a one-and-a-half story home whose exterior is distinctive. It has a contemporary feeling, yet it retains some of the fine design features and proportions of traditional exteriors. Inside the appealing double front doors there is livability galore. The sunken rear living-dining area is delightfully spacious and is looked down into from the second floor lounge. The open end fireplace, with its raised hearth and planter, is another focal point. The master bedroom features a fine compartmented bath with both shower and tub. The study is just a couple steps away. The U-shaped kitchen is outstanding. Notice the pantry and laundry. Upstairs provides children with their own sleeping, studying and TV quarters. Absolutely a great design! Study all the fine details closely with your family.

Design 122780

2,006 Sq. Ft. - First Floor
718 Sq. Ft. - Second Floor; 42,110 Cu. Ft.

● This 1½-story contemporary has more fine features than one can imagine. The livability is outstanding and can be appreciated by the whole family. Note the fine indoor-outdoor living relationships.

Design 122772

1,579 Sq. Ft. - First Floor
1,240 Sq. Ft. - Second Floor; 39,460 Cu. Ft.

● This four-bedroom two-story contemporary design is sure to suit your growing family needs. The rear U-shaped kitchen, flanked by the family and dining rooms, will be very efficient to the busy homemaker. Parents will enjoy all the convenience of the master bedroom suite.

Design 122771

2,087 Sq. Ft. - First Floor
816 Sq. Ft. - Second Floor; 53,285 Cu. Ft.

● This design will provide an abundance of livability for your family. The second floor is highlighted by an open lounge which overlooks both the entry and the gathering room below.

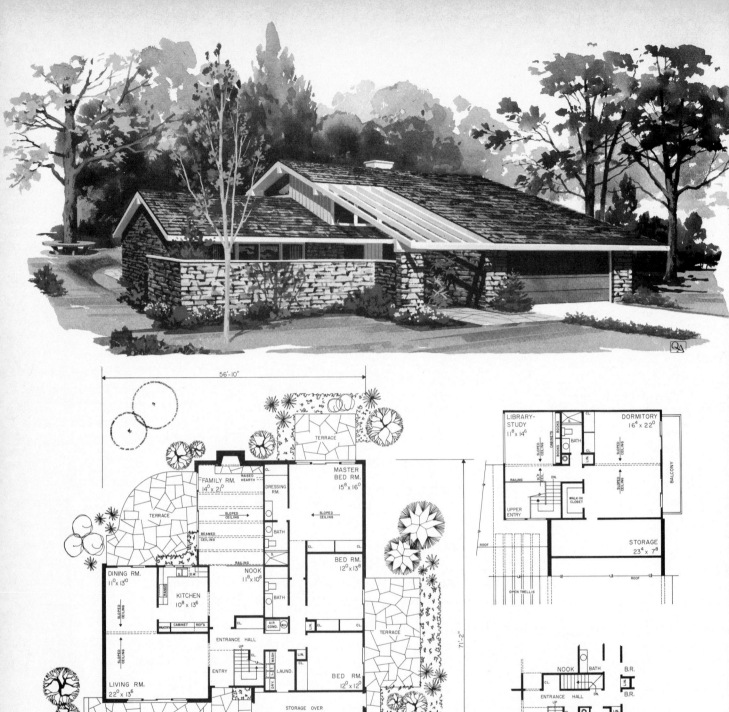

Design 122340
2,310 Sq. Ft. - First Floor
763 Sq. Ft. - Second Floor
32,460 Cu. Ft.

● If you have a flair for the extraordinary and wish to introduce your family to living patterns that will be delightfully different, then this design should fill the bill. Whether you build with quarried stone, brick veneer or some other exterior material of your choice, you'll surely experience pride of ownership here. However, inside is where your family's fun really begins. This is a highly integrated plan which allows for the full expression of a family's diverse activities. Study the effective zoning of the first floor.

There are the formal, the informal and the sleeping areas. Then, upstairs there is a library which can look down on the entrance hall. Also, the dormitory with its own bath, balcony and fine closet facilities. Note optional basement. Laundry remains upstairs.

Design 122582
1,195 Sq. Ft. - First Floor
731 Sq. Ft. - Second Floor
32,500 Cu. Ft.

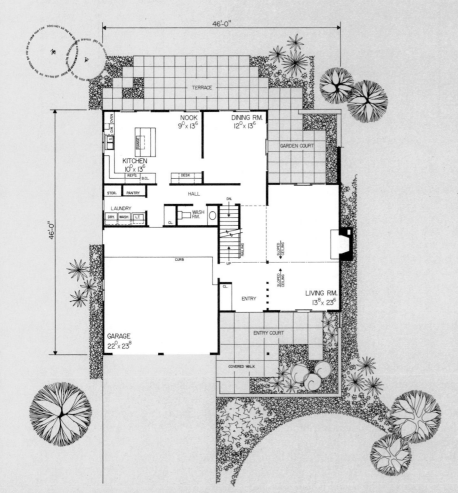

● This distinctive two-story will command attention wherever built. One of its significant features is that it doesn't require a huge piece of property. In slightly less than 2,000 square feet it offers tremendous livability. As a bonus, the basement can function as the family recreation and hobby areas. Of particular interest is the first floor laundry room. Don't miss the fine kitchen layout, the formal and informal dining facilities and the sloping ceiling of the living room. Notice the outstanding outdoor living facilities. Upstairs, three bedrooms and two baths will be found.

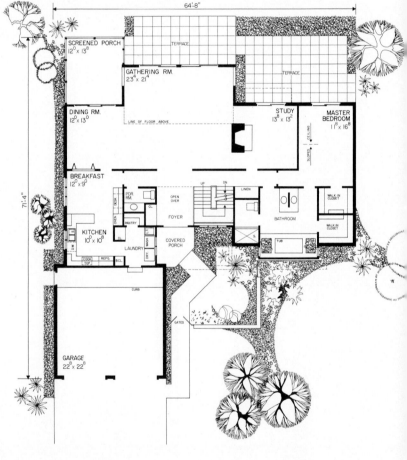

Design 122581

2,125 Sq. Ft. - First Floor
903 Sq. Ft. - Second Floor
54,476 Cu. Ft.

● A study with a fireplace! What a fine attraction to find in this lovely three-bedroom home. And the fine features certainly do not stop there. The gathering room has a sloped ceiling and two sliding glass doors to the rear terrace. The study and master bedroom (which has first floor privacy and convenience) also have glass doors to the wrap-around terrace. Adjacent to the gathering room is a formal dining room and screened-in porch. The efficient kitchen with its many built-ins has easy access to the first floor laundry. The separate breakfast nook has a built-in desk. The second floor has two bedrooms each having at least one walk-in closet. Also, a lounge overlooking the gathering room below and a balcony. Note the oversized two-car garage for storing bikes and lawn mowers. The front courtyard adds a measure of privacy to the covered porch entrance.

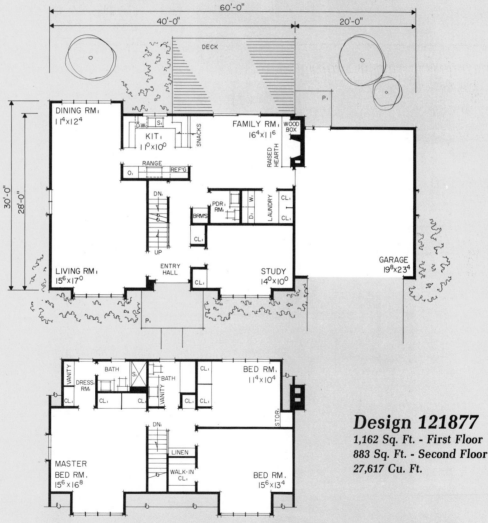

Design 121877
1,162 Sq. Ft. - First Floor
883 Sq. Ft. - Second Floor
27,617 Cu. Ft.

● This simple, straightforward plan has much to offer in the way of livability and economical construction costs. Worthy of particular note are the excellent traffic patterns and the outstanding use of space. There is no wasted space here. Notice the cozy family room with its raised hearth fireplace, wood box and sliding glass doors to the sweeping outdoor deck. The efficient kitchen is flanked by the informal snack bar and the formal dining area. Open planning between the living and dining areas promotes a fine feeling of spaciousness. The study is a great feature. It may function as just that or become, the sewing or TV room, the guest room or even the fourth bedroom. Note the powder room and laundry. Study the second floor facilities.

Design 122884 1,855 Sq. Ft. - First Floor
837 Sq. Ft. - Second Floor; 50,137 Cu. Ft.

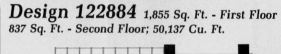

● The greenhouse in this design enhances its energy-efficiency and allows for spacious and interesting living patterns. Being a one-and-a-half story design, the second floor could be developed at a later date when the space is needed. The greenhouses add an additional 418 sq. ft. and 8,793 cu. ft. to the above quoted figures.

Design 122831

1,758 Sq. Ft. - First Floor
1,247 Sq. Ft. - Second Floor
44,265 Cu. Ft.

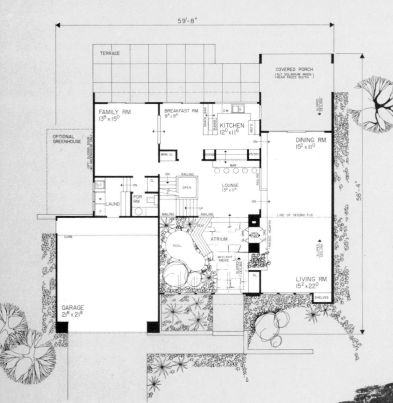

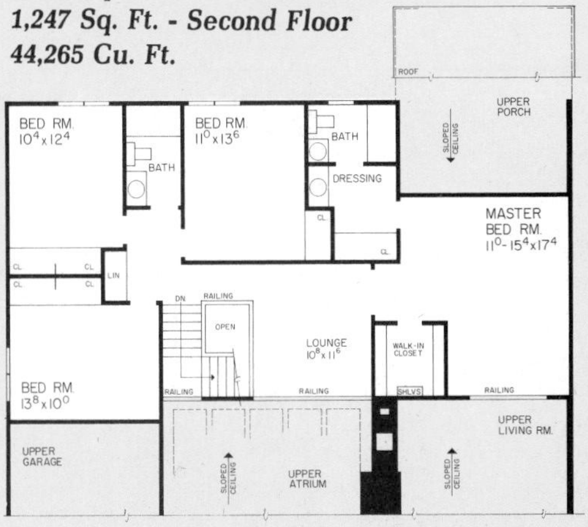

FIRST FLOOR plan labels:
TERRACE
COVERED PORCH (ALT SOLARIUM WHEN REAR FACES SOUTH)
FAMILY RM. 13⁸ x 15⁰
BREAKFAST RM. 9⁴ x 9⁶
KITCHEN 12⁰ x 11⁶
DINING RM. 15² x 11⁰
OPTIONAL GREENHOUSE
LOUNGE 13² x 11⁶
LAUND
PDR RM.
ATRIUM
POOL
SKYLIGHT ABOVE
RAISED HEARTH
LINE OF SECOND FLR.
LIVING RM. 15² x 22⁰
SHELVES
GARAGE 21⁸ x 21⁸
59'-8"
58'-4"

SECOND FLOOR plan labels:
ROOF
UPPER PORCH
BED RM. 10⁴ x 12⁴
BED RM. 11⁰ x 13⁶
BATH
DRESSING
MASTER BED RM. 11⁰-15⁴ x 17⁴
BED RM. 13⁸ x 10⁰
OPEN
LOUNGE 10⁸ x 11⁶
WALK-IN CLOSET
UPPER GARAGE
UPPER ATRIUM
UPPER LIVING RM.

● You can incorporate energy-saving features into the elevation of this passive solar design to enable you to receive the most sunlight on your particular site. Multiple plot plans (included with the blueprints) illustrate which elevations should be solarized for different sites and which extra features can be incorporated. The features can include a greenhouse added to the family room, the back porch turned into a solarium or skylights installed over the entry.

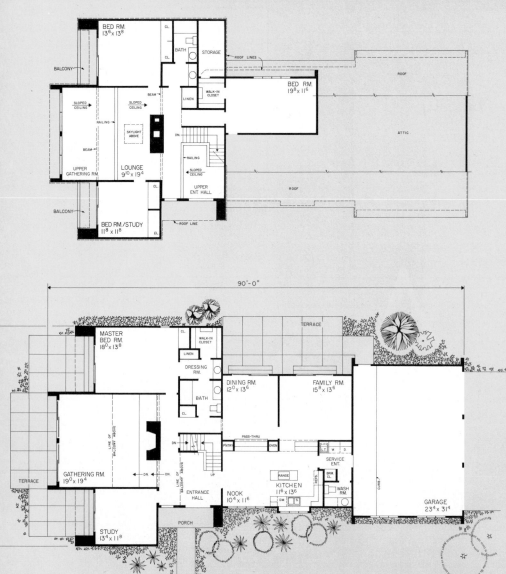

Design 122781

2,132 Sq. Ft. - First Floor
1,156 Sq. Ft. - Second Floor
47,365 Cu. Ft.

● This beautifully designed two-story could be considered a dream house of a
lifetime. The exterior is
sure to catch the eye of
anyone who takes sight of
its unique construction.
The front kitchen features
an island range, adjacent
breakfast nook and pass-
thru to formal dining room.
The master bedroom suite
with its privacy and con-
venience on the first floor
has a spacious walk-in
closet and dressing room.
The side terrace is accessible through sliding glass
doors from the master bedroom, gathering room and
study. The second floor has
three bedrooms and storage
space galore. Also notice
the lounge which has a
sloped ceiling and a sky-
light above. This delightful
area looks down into the
gathering room. The out-
door balconies overlook the
wrap-around terrace. Surely an outstanding trend
house for decades to come.

Design 122782
2,060 Sq. Ft. - First Floor
897 Sq. Ft. - Second Floor
47,750 Cu. Ft.

● What makes this such a distinctive four bedroom design? Let's list some of the features. This plan includes great formal and informal living for the family at home or when entertaining guests. The formal gathering room and informal family room share a dramatic raised hearth fireplace. Other features of the sunken gathering room include: high, sloped ceilings, built-in planter and sliding glass doors to the front entrance court. The kitchen has a snack bar, many built-ins, a pass-thru to dining room and easy access to the large laundry/washroom. The master bedroom suite is located on the main level for added privacy and convenience. There's even a study with a built-in bar. The upper level has three more bedrooms, a bath and a lounge looking down into the gathering room.

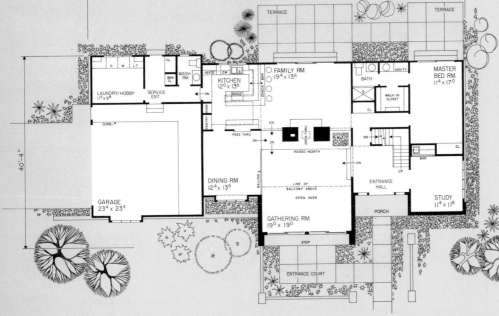

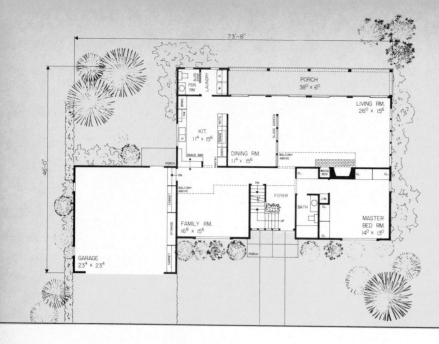

Design 122246 1,651 Sq. Ft. - First Floor
1,161 Sq. Ft. - Second Floor; 52,382 Cu. Ft.

● This contemporary design has a trace of chalet in its ancestry. Sloping ceilings, open planning and plenty of glass assure an atmosphere of spaciousness throughout the interior.

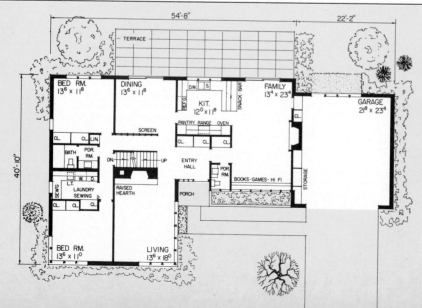

● A terrific contemporary design! Four bedrooms, 3½ baths, formal and informal living are planned for efficient living.

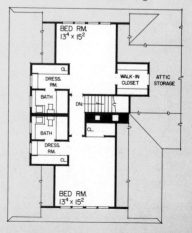

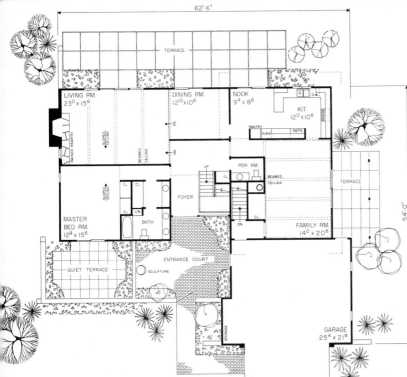

This refreshing design has just enough individuality - both inside and out - to assure its own full measure of distinction. Sliding glass doors provide the living, dining and family rooms with direct access to their own terrace areas. You can look down into the foyer and the dining room from the second floor.

Design 122252
1,810 Sq. Ft. - First Floor
1,033 Sq. Ft. - Second Floor; 38,346 Cu. Ft.

Design 121084
1,804 Sq. Ft. - First Floor
732 Sq. Ft. - Second Floor
33,842 Cu. Ft.

Design 122377

1,170 Sq. Ft. - First Floor
815 Sq. Ft. - Second Floor
22,477 Cu. Ft.

● What an impressive up-to-date home this is. Its refreshing configuration will command a full measure of attention. Note that all of the back rooms on the first floor are a couple steps lower than the entry and living room area. Separating the living room and the slightly lower level is a thru-fireplace which has a raised hearth in the family room. An adjacent planter with vertical members provides additional interest and beauty. The rear terrace is accessible from nook, family and dining rooms. Four bedrooms serviced by two full baths comprise the second floor which looks down into the living room. A large walk-in storage closet will be ideal for those seasonal items. An attractive outdoor planter extends across the rear just outside the bedroom windows. This will surely be a house that will be fun in which to live.

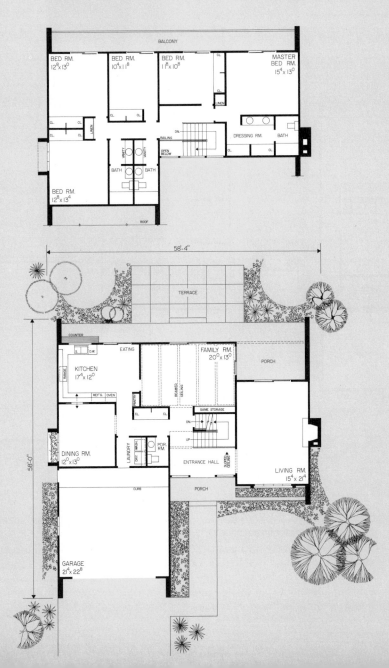

Design 122390

1,368 Sq. Ft. - First Floor
1,428 Sq. Ft. - Second Floor
37,734 Cu. Ft.

● If yours is a large family and you like the architecture of the Far West don't look further. Particularly if you envision building on a modest sized lot. Projecting the garage to the front contributes to the drama of this contemporary two-story. Its stucco exterior is beautifully enhanced by the clay tiles of the varying roof surfaces. Inside the double front doors is just about everything a large, active family would require for pleasurable, convenient living. The focal point, of course, is the five bedroom (count'em), three bath second floor. Four bedrooms have access to the outdoor balcony. The first floor offers two large living areas - the formal living and the informal family rooms - plus, two eating areas. Although there is the basement, the laundry is on the first floor. Don't overlook the covered porch accessible by family and living rooms.

Design 122339 2,068 Sq. Ft. - First Floor; 589 Sq. Ft. - Second Floor; 27,950 Cu. Ft.

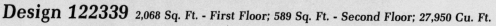

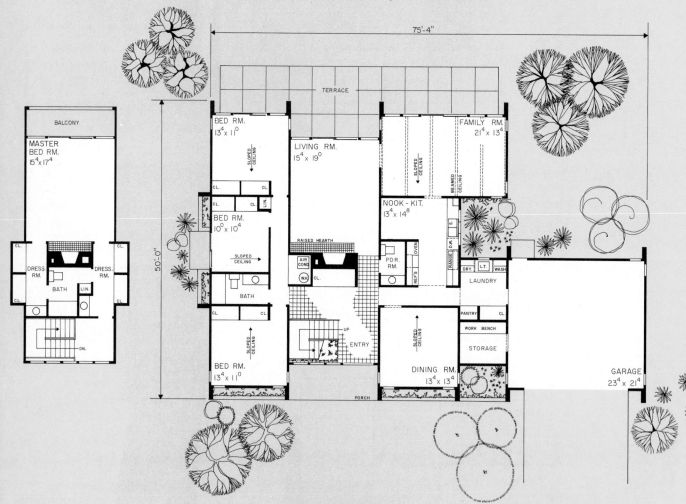

75'-4"

50'-0"

TERRACE

BALCONY

MASTER BED RM. 15⁴ x 17⁴

BED RM. 13⁴ x 11⁰

LIVING RM. 15⁴ x 19⁰

FAMILY RM. 21⁴ x 13⁴

SLOPED CEILING

BEAMED CEILING

CL. CL. LIN.

DRESS. RM.

DRESS. RM.

BATH LIN.

BED RM. 10⁰ x 10⁴

SLOPED CEILING

NOOK - KIT. 13⁴ x 14⁸

RANGE D.W.

REF'G. OVEN

PDR. RM.

RAISED HEARTH

AIR COND.

WH

CL.

BATH

DRY. L.T. WASH

LAUNDRY

DN.

CL.

BED RM. 13⁴ x 11⁰

SLOPED CEILING

UP

ENTRY

SLOPED CEILING

PANTRY CL.

WORK BENCH

STORAGE

GARAGE 23⁴ x 21⁴

PORCH

DINING RM. 13⁴ x 13⁴

● Here, the influence of the Spanish Southwest comes into clear view. The smooth texture of the stucco exterior contrasts pleasingly with the roughness of the tile roofs. Contributing to the appeal of this contemporary design are the varying roof planes, the interesting angles and the blank wall masses punctuated by the glass areas. Whether called upon to function as a two-story home, or a one-story ranch with an attic studio, this design will deliver interesting and enjoyable living patterns. Sloping ceilings and generous glass areas foster a feeling of spaciousness. Traffic patterns are excellent and the numerous storage facilities are outstanding. Fireplaces are the focal point of the living room and the second floor master bedroom. Three more bedrooms are on the first floor.

Design 122309 1,719 Sq. Ft. - First Floor; 456 Sq. Ft. - Second Floor; 22,200 Cu. Ft.

● Here's proof that the simple rectangle (which is relatively economical to build, naturally) can, when properly planned, result in unique living patterns. The exterior can be exceedingly appealing, too. Study the floor plan carefully. The efficiency of the kitchen could hardly be improved upon. It is strategically located to serve the formal dining room, the family room and even the rear terrace. The sleeping facilities are arranged in a most interesting manner. The master bedroom with its attached bath and dressing room will enjoy a full measure of privacy on the first floor. A second bedroom is also on this floor and has a full bath nearby. Upstairs there are two more bedrooms and a bath. Don't miss the laundry, the snack bar, the beamed ceiling or the sliding glass doors.

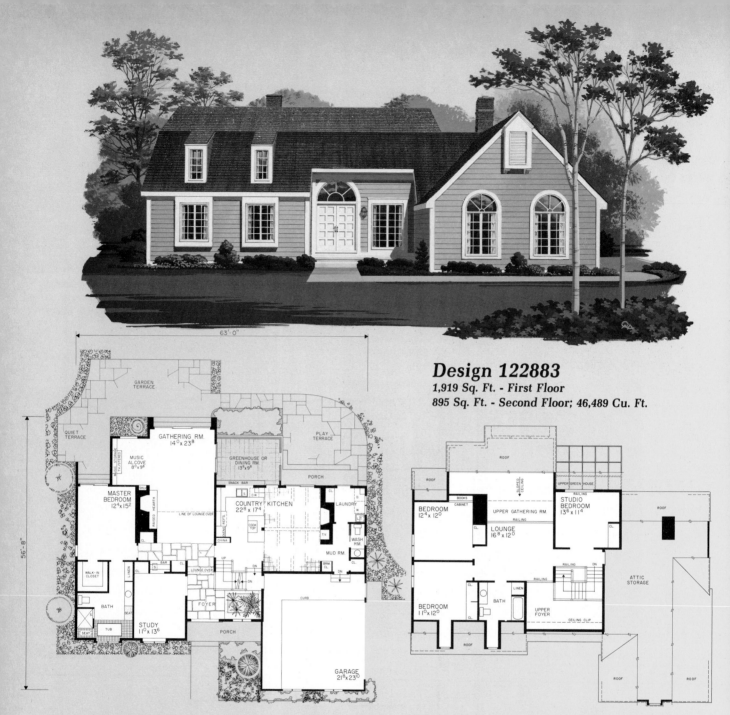

Design 122883

1,919 Sq. Ft. - First Floor
895 Sq. Ft. - Second Floor; 46,489 Cu. Ft.

● A country-style home is part of America's fascination with the rural past. This home's emphasis of the traditional home is in its gambrel roof, dormers and fanlight windows. Having a traditional exterior from the street view, this home has window walls and a greenhouse, which opens the house to the outdoors in a thoroughly contemporary manner. The interior meets the requirements of today's active family. Like the country houses of the past, it has a gathering room for family get-togethers or entertaining. The adjacent two-story greenhouse doubles as the dining room. There is a pass-thru snack bar to the country kitchen here. This country kitchen just might be the heart of the house with its two areas - work zone and sitting room. There are four bedrooms on the two floors - the master bedroom suite on the first floor; three more on the second floor. A lounge, overlooking the gathering room and front foyer, is also on the second floor.

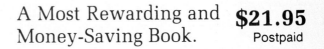
Contents

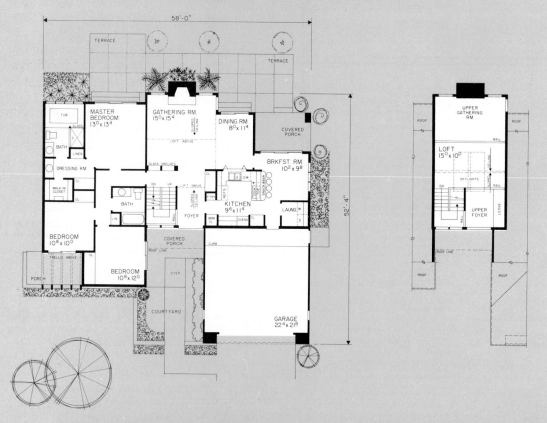

Design 122892 *1,623 Sq. Ft. - First Floor; 160 Sq. Ft. - Second Floor; 38,670 Cu. Ft.*

● What a striking contemporary! It houses an efficient floor plan with many outstanding features. The foyer has a sloped ceiling and an open staircase to the basement. To the right of the foyer is the work center. Note the snack bar, laundry and covered dining porch, along with the step-saving kitchen. Both the gathering and dining rooms overlook the back yard. Each of the three bedrooms has access to an outdoor area. Now, just think of the potential use of the second floor loft. It could be used as a den, sewing room, lounge, TV room or anything else you may need. It overlooks the gathering room and front foyer. Two large skylights will brighten the interior.

Design 122887 *1,338 Sq. Ft. - First Floor; 661 Sq. Ft. - Second Floor; 36,307 Cu. Ft.*

● This attractive, contemporary one-and-a-half story will be the envy of many. First, examine the efficient kitchen. Not only does it offer a snack bar for those quick meals but also a large dining room. Notice the adjacent dining porch. The laundry and garage access are also adjacent to the kitchen.

An exciting feature is the gathering room with fireplace. The first floor also offers a study with a wet bar and sliding glass doors that open to a private porch. This will make those quiet times cherishable. Adjacent to the study is a full bath followed by a bedroom. Upstairs a large master bedroom suite oc-

cupies the entire floor. It features a bath with an oversized tub and shower, a large walk-in closet with built-ins and an open lounge with fireplace. Both the lounge and master bedroom, along with the gathering room, have sloped ceilings. Develop the lower level for additional space.

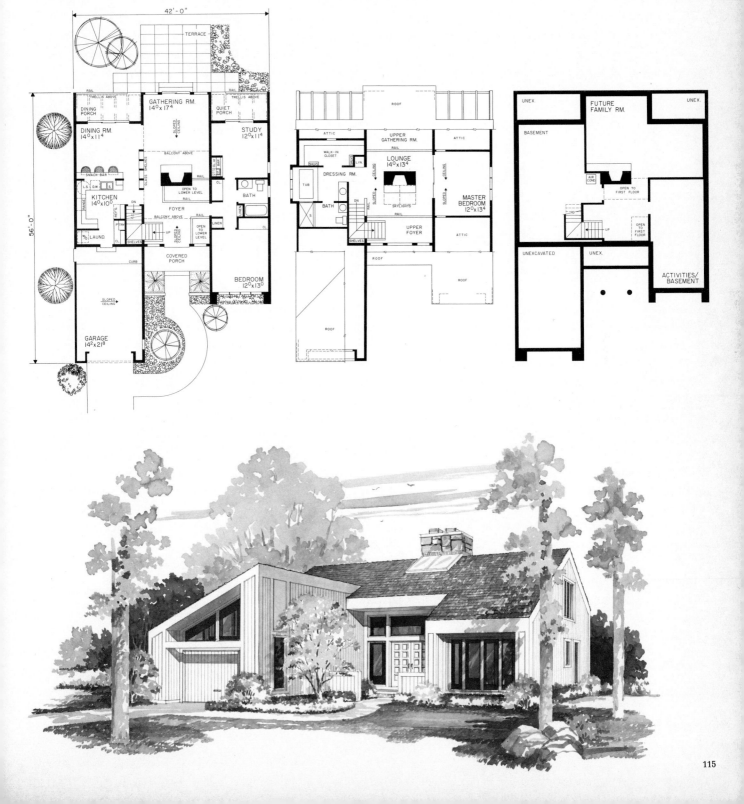

Design 122900 2,332 Sq. Ft. - First Floor;

953 Sq. Ft. - Second Floor; 46,677 Cu. Ft.

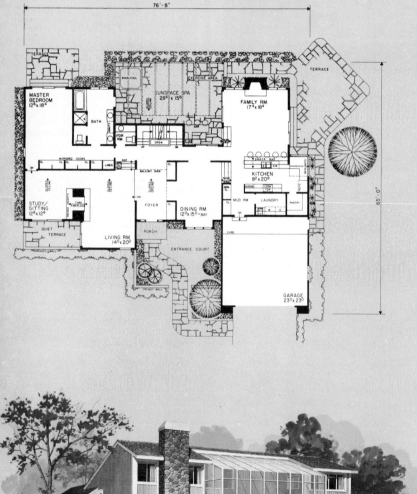

● Contemporary in exterior styling, this house is energy oriented. It calls for 2 x 6 exterior wall construction with placement on a north facing lot. Traffic flows through the interior of this plan by way of the foyer. Not only is the foyer useful, but it is dramatic with its sloped ceiling and second floor balcony and skylight above. Excellent living areas are throughout. A spacious, sunken living room is to the left of the foyer. It shares a thru-fireplace, faced with fieldstone, with the study. Sloped ceilings are in both of these rooms. Informal activities can take place in the family room. It, too, has a fireplace and is adjacent to the work center. Two of the bedrooms are on the second floor with a lounge overlooking the gathering room below. The master bedroom is on the first floor. A generous amount of closet space with mirrored doors will enhance its appearance. Study the spacious master bath with all of its many features. Its direct access to the sunspace spa will be appreciated.

All The "TOOLS" You And Your Builder Need. . .

1. THE PLAN BOOKS

Home Planners' unique Design Category Series makes it easy to look at and study only the types of designs for which you and your family have an interest. Each of six plan books features a specific type of home, namely: Two-Story, 1½ Story, One-Story Over 2000 Sq. Ft., One-Story Under 2000 Sq. Ft., Multi-Levels and Vacation Homes. In addition to the convenient Design Category Series, there is an impressive selection of other current titles. While the home plans featured in these books are also to be found in the Design Category Series, they, too, are edited for those with special tastes and requirements. Your family will spend many enjoyable hours reviewing the delightfully designed exteriors and the practical floor plans. Surely your home or office library should include a selection of these popular plan books. Your complete satisfaction is guaranteed.

2. THE CONSTRUCTION BLUEPRINTS

There are blueprints available for each of the designs published in Home Planners' current plan books. Depending upon the size, the style and the type of home, each set of blueprints consists of from five to ten large sheets. Only by studying the blueprints is it possible to give complete and final consideration to the proper selection of a design for your next home. The blueprints provide the opportunity for all family members to familiarize themselves with the features of all exterior elevations, interior elevations and details, all dimensions, special built-in features and effects. They also provide a full understanding of the materials to be used and/or selected. The low-cost of our blueprints makes it possible and indeed, practical, to study in detail a number of different sets of blueprints before deciding upon which design to build.

3. THE MATERIALS LIST

A list of materials is an integral part of the plan package. It comprises the last sheet of each set of blueprints and serves as a handy reference during the period of construction. Of course, at the pricing and the material ordering stages, it is indispensable.

4. THE SPECIFICATION OUTLINE

Each order for blueprints is accompanied by one Specification Outline. You and your builder will find this a time-saving tool when deciding upon your own individual specifications. An important reference document should you wish to write your own specifications.

5. THE PLUMBING & ELECTRICAL PACKAGE

The construction blueprints you order from Home Planners, Inc. include locations for all plumbing fixtures — sinks, lavatories, tubs, showers, water closets, laundry trays, hot water heaters, etc. The blueprints also show the locations of all electrical switches, plugs, and outlets. These plumbing and electrical details are sufficient to present to your local contractor for discussions about your individual specifications and subsequent installations in conformance with local codes. However, for those who wish to acquaint themselves with many of the intricacies of residential plumbing and electrical details and installations, Home Planners, Inc. has made available this package. We do not recommend that the layman attempt to do his own plumbing and electrical work. It is, nevertheless, advisable that owners be as knowledgeable as possible about each of these disciplines. The entire family will appreciate the educational value of these low-cost, easy-to-understand details.

The Design Category Series

1.

360 TWO STORY HOMES

English Tudors, Early American Salt Boxes, Gambrels, Farmhouses, Southern Colonials, Georgians, French Mansards, Contemporaries. Interesting floor plans for both small and large families. Efficient kitchens, 2 to 6 bedrooms, family rooms, libraries, extra baths, mud rooms. Homes for all budgets.

288 Pages, $6.95

2.

150 1½ STORY HOMES

Cape Cod, Williamsburg, Georgian, Tudor and Contemporary versions. Low budget and country-estate feature sections. Expandable family plans. Formal and informal living and dining areas along with gathering rooms. Spacious, country kitchens. Indoor-outdoor livability with covered porches and functional terraces.

128 Pages, $3.95

3.

210 ONE STORY HOMES OVER 2,000 Sq. Ft.

All popular styles. Including Spanish, Western, Tudor French, and other traditional versions. Contemporaries Gracious, family living patterns. Sunken living rooms master bedroom suites, atriums, courtyards, pools. Fine indoor-outdoor living relationships. For modest to country-estate budgets.

192 Pages, $4.95

4.

315 ONE STORY HOMES UNDER 2,000 Sq. Ft.

A great selection of traditional and contemporary exteriors for medium and restricted budgets. Efficient, practical floor plans. Gathering rooms, formal and informal living and dining rooms, mud rooms, indoor-outdoor livability. Economically built homes. Designs with bonus space livability for growing families.

192 Pages, $4.95

5.

215 MULTI-LEVEL HOMES

For new dimensions in family living. A captivating variety of exterior styles, exciting floor plans for flat and sloping sites. Exposed lower levels. Balconies, decks. Plans for the active family. Upper level lounges, excellent bath facilities. Sloping ceilings. Functional outdoor terraces. For all building budgets.

192 Pages, $4.95

6.

223 VACATION HOMES

Features A-Frames, Chalets Hexagons, economical rectangles. One and two stories plus multi-levels. Lodges for year 'round livability. From 480 to 3238 sq. ft. Cottages sleeping 2 to 22. For flat or sloping sites Spacious, open planning. Over 600 illustrations. 120 Pages in full color. Cluster homes selection. For lakeshore or woodland leisure living.

176 Pages, $4.95

The Exterior Style Series

7.

330 EARLY AMERICAN PLANS

Our new *Essential Guide to Early American Home Plans* traces Early American architecture from our Colonial Past to Traditional styles popular today with a written history of designs and colorful sections devoted to styles. Many of our designs are patterned after historic homes.

304 Pages, $9.95

8.

335 CONTEMPORARY HOME PLANS

Our new *Essential Guide to Contemporary Home Plans* offers a colorful directory to modern architecture, including a history of American Contemporary styling and more than 335 home plans of all sizes and popular designs. 304 colorful pages! Must reading for contemporary lifestyles.

304 Pages, $9.95

9.

135 ENGLISH TUDOR HOMES

and other Popular Family Plans is a favorite of many The current popularity of the English Tudor home design i phenomenal. Here is a book which is loaded with Tudor for all budgets. There are one-story, 1½ and two-story designs, plus multi-levels and hillsides from 1,176-3,849 sq. ft.

104 Pages, $3.95

The Budget Series

11.

175 LOW BUDGET HOMES

A special selection of home designs for the modest or restricted building budget. An excellent variety of Traditional and Contemporary designs. One-story, 1½ and two-story and split-level homes. Three, four and five bedrooms. Family rooms, extra baths, formal and informal dining rooms. Basement and non-basement designs. Attached garages and covered porches.

96 Pages, $2.95

12.

165 AFFORDABLE HOME PLANS

This outstanding book was specially edited with a wide selection of houses and plans for those with a medium building budget. While none of these designs are considered low-cost; neither do they require an unlimited budget to build. Square footages range from 1,428. Exteriors of Tudor, French, Early American, Spanish and Contemporary are included.

112 Pages, $2.95

13.

142 HOME DESIGNS FOR EXPANDED BUILDING BUDGETS

A family's ability to finance and need for a larger home grows as its size and income increases. This selection highlights designs which house an average square footage of 2,551. One-story plans average 2,069; two-stories, 2,735 multi-levels, 2,825. Spacious homes featuring raised hearth fireplaces, open planning and efficient kitchens.

112 Pages, $2.95

General Interest Titles

ENCYCLOPEDIA - 450 PLANS

For those who wish to review and study perhaps the largest selection of designs available in a single volume. Varying exterior styles, plus interesting and practical floor plans for all building budgets. Formal, informal living patterns; indoor-outdoor livability; small, growing and large family facilities.

15.

320 Pages, $9.95

244 HOUSE PLANS FOR BETTER LIVING

Special 40th Anniversary Edition with over 650 illustrations. Sectionalized to highlight special interest groups of designs. A fine introduction to our special interest titles. All styles, sizes, and types of homes are represented. Designs feature gathering rooms, country kitchens, second-floor lounges.

16.

192 Pages $3.50

255 HOME DESIGNS FOR FAMILY LIVING

In addition to the plans that cater to a variety of family living patterns and budgets, there are special sections on vacation homes, earth-sheltered homes, sun-oriented living, and shared livability. One, 1½, two-story, and multi-level designs. The book includes over 700 illustrations.

17.

192 Pages, $3.50

COLOR PORTFOLIO - 310 DESIGNS

An expanded full-color guide to our most popular Early American, Spanish, French, Tudor, Contemporary, and modern Trend home designs. 310 home plans of all popular styles and sizes. Includes energy-efficient designs. Plans for varying building budgets. One, 1½, two-story, and split-level designs for all terrain. This is our largest full-color book with our newest trend-setting designs and other favorites. It's must reading for the serious home planner.

18.

288 Pages in Full Color, $12.95

136 SPANISH & WESTERN HOME DESIGNS

Stucco exteriors, arches, tile roofs, wide-overhangs, courtyards and rambling ranches are characteristics which make this design selection distinctive. These sun-country designs highlight indoor-outdoor relationships. Solar oriented livability is featured.

10.

120 Pages, $3.95

PLAN BOOKS are a valuable tool for anyone who plans to build a new home. After you have selected a home design that satisfies your list of requirements, you can order blueprints for further study.

115 HOME DESIGNS FOR UNLIMITED BUILDING BUDGETS

This book will appeal to those with large families and the desire and wherewithal to satisfy all the family needs, plus most of their wants. The upscale designs in this portfolio average 3,132 square feet. One-story designs average 2,796 sq. ft.; 1½-story, 3,188 sq. ft.; two-story, 3,477 sq. ft.; multi-level, 3,532 sq. ft. Truly designs for elegant living.

14.

112 Pages, $2.95

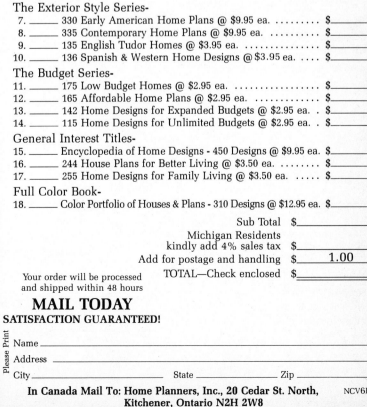

HOME PLANNERS, INC.
Dept. BK, 23761 Research Drive
Farmington Hills, Michigan 48024

Please mail me the following:

THE DESIGN CATEGORY SERIES - A great series of books specially edited by design type and size. Each book features interesting sections to further enhance the study of design styles, sizes and house types. A fine addition to the home or office library. Complete collection - over 1250 designs.

1. _____ 360 Two Story Homes @ $6.95 ea. .... $_____
2. _____ 150 1½ Story Homes @ $3.95 ea. .... $_____
3. _____ 210 One Story Homes - Over 2,000 Sq. Ft. @ $4.95 ea. . $_____
4. _____ 315 One Story Homes - Under 2,000 Sq. Ft. @ $4.95 ea. $_____
5. _____ 215 Multi-Level Homes @ $4.95 ea. .... $_____
6. _____ 223 Vacation Homes @ $4.95 ea. .... $_____

OTHER CURRENT TITLES - The interesting series of plan books listed below have been edited to appeal to various style preferences and budget considerations. The majority of the designs highlighted in these books also may be found in the Design Category Series.

The Exterior Style Series-
7. _____ 330 Early American Home Plans @ $9.95 ea. .... $_____
8. _____ 335 Contemporary Home Plans @ $9.95 ea. .... $_____
9. _____ 135 English Tudor Homes @ $3.95 ea. .... $_____
10. _____ 136 Spanish & Western Home Designs @ $3.95 ea. .... $_____

The Budget Series-
11. _____ 175 Low Budget Homes @ $2.95 ea. .... $_____
12. _____ 165 Affordable Home Plans @ $2.95 ea. .... $_____
13. _____ 142 Home Designs for Expanded Budgets @ $2.95 ea. . $_____
14. _____ 115 Home Designs for Unlimited Budgets @ $2.95 ea. . $_____

General Interest Titles-
15. _____ Encyclopedia of Home Designs - 450 Designs @ $9.95 ea. $_____
16. _____ 244 House Plans for Better Living @ $3.50 ea. .... $_____
17. _____ 255 Home Designs for Family Living @ $3.50 ea. ..... $_____

Full Color Book-
18. _____ Color Portfolio of Houses & Plans - 310 Designs @ $12.95 ea. $_____

Sub Total $_____
Michigan Residents kindly add 4% sales tax $_____
Add for postage and handling $___1.00___
TOTAL—Check enclosed $_____

Your order will be processed and shipped within 48 hours

MAIL TODAY
SATISFACTION GUARANTEED!

Please Print

Name _____
Address _____
City _____ State _____ Zip _____

In Canada Mail To: Home Planners, Inc., 20 Cedar St. North, Kitchener, Ontario N2H 2W8

NCV6BK

Frontal
Sheet

Foundation
Plans

Detailed
Floor
Plans

House
Cross-
Sections

Interior
Elevations

Exterior
Elevations

Material
List

The Blueprints

1. FRONTAL SHEET.
Artist's landscaped sketch of the exterior and ink-line floor plans are on the frontal sheet of each set of blueprints.

2. FOUNDATION PLAN.
¼" Scale basement and foundation plan. All necessary notations and dimensions. Plot plan diagram for locating house on building site.

3. DETAILED FLOOR PLAN.
¼" Scale first and second floor plans with complete dimensions. Cross-section detail keys. Diagrammatic layout of electrical outlets and switches.

4. HOUSE CROSS-SECTIONS.
Large scale sections of foundation, interior and exterior walls, floors and roof details for design and construction control.

5. INTERIOR ELEVATIONS.
Large scale interior details of the complete kitchen cabinet design, bathrooms, powder room, laundry, fireplaces, paneling, beam ceilings, built-in cabinets, etc.

6. EXTERIOR ELEVATIONS.
¼" Scale exterior elevation drawings of front, rear, and both sides of the house. All exterior materials and details are shown to indicate the complete design and proportions of the house.

7. MATERIAL LIST.
Complete lists of all materials required for the construction of the house as designed are included in each set of blueprints.

THIS BLUEPRINT PACKAGE
will help you and your family take a major step forward in the final appraisal and planning of your new home. Only by spending many enjoyable and informative hours studying the numerous details included in the complete package, will you feel sure of, and comfortable with, your commitment to build your new home. To assure successful and productive consultation with your builder and/or architect, reference to the various elements of the blueprint package is a must. The blueprints, material list and specification outline will save much consultation time and expense. Don't be without them.

The Material List

With each set of blueprints you order you will receive a material list. Each list shows you the quantity, type and size of the non-mechanical materials required to build your home. It also tells you where these materials are used. This makes the blueprints easy to understand.

Influencing the mechanical requirements are geographical differences in availability of materials, local codes, methods of installation and individual preferences. Because of these factors, your local heating, plumbing and electrical contractors can supply you with necessary material take-offs for their particular trades.

Material lists simplify your material ordering and enable you to get quicker price quotations from your builder and material dealer. Because the material list is an integral part of each set of blueprints, it is not available separately.

Among the materials listed:

• Masonry, Veneer & Fireplace • Framing Lumber • Roofing & Sheet Metal • Windows & Door Frames • Exterior Trim & Insulation • Tile Work, Finish Floors • Interior Trim, Kitchen Cabinets • Rough & Finish Hardware

The Specification Outline

This fill-in type specification lists over 150 phases of home construction from excavating to painting and includes wiring, plumbing, heating and air-conditioning. It consists of 16 pages and will prove invaluable for specifying to your builder the exact materials, equipment and methods of construction you want in your new home. One Specification Outline is included free with each order for blueprints. Additional Specification Outlines are available at $3.00 each.

CONTENTS
• General Instructions, Suggestions and Information • Excavating and Grading • Masonry and Concrete Work • Sheet Metal Work • Carpentry, Millwork, Roofing, and Miscellaneous Items • Lath and Plaster or Drywall Wallboard • Schedule for Room Finishes • Painting and Finishing • Tile Work • Electrical Work • Plumbing • Heating and Air-Conditioning

The Plumbing & Electrical Package

Consists of Large 24" x 36" Sheets for Easy Reference.
Color-Coded for Quick Recognition
of Details.

For those who wish to acquaint themselves
with many of the intricacies of
residential plumbing and electrical
details and installations.
An invaluable tool and
great supplement to
the blueprint
package.

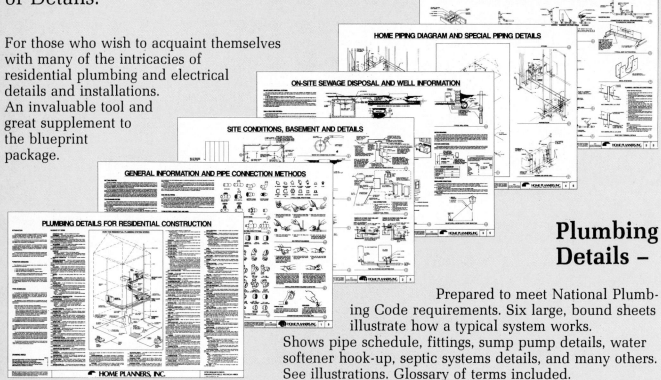

Plumbing Details –

Prepared to meet National Plumbing Code requirements. Six large, bound sheets illustrate how a typical system works.
Shows pipe schedule, fittings, sump pump details, water softener hook-up, septic systems details, and many others.
See illustrations. Glossary of terms included.

Only $12.95

Of Great Educational Value to the Entire Family.
Order Both Sets

only
$19.95
(Save $5.95)

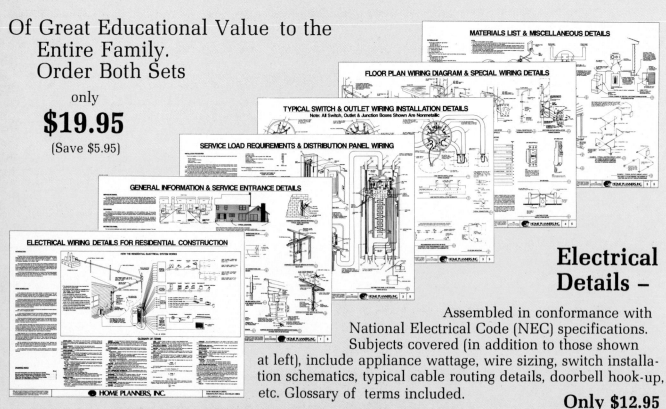

Electrical Details –

Assembled in conformance with National Electrical Code (NEC) specifications. Subjects covered (in addition to those shown at left), include appliance wattage, wire sizing, switch installation schematics, typical cable routing details, doorbell hook-up, etc. Glossary of terms included.

Only $12.95

To order, see form on next page.

Before You Order

1. STUDY THE DESIGNS . . . found in Home Planners books. As you review these delightful custom homes, you should keep in mind the total living requirements of your family — both indoors and outdoors. Although we do not make changes in plans, many minor changes can be made prior to the period of construction. If major changes are involved to satisfy your personal requirements, you should consider ordering one set of blueprints and having them redrawn locally. Consultation with your architect is strongly advised when contemplating major changes.

2. HOW TO ORDER BLUEPRINTS . . . After you have chosen the design that satisfies your requirements, or if you have selected one that you wish to study in more detail, simply clip the accompanying order blank and mail with your remittance. However, if it is not convenient for you to send a check or money order, you can use your credit card, or merely indicate C.O.D. shipment. Postman will collect all charges, including postage and C.O.D. fee C.O.D. shipments are not permitted to Canada or foreign countries. Should time be of essence, as it sometimes is with many of our customers, your telephone order usually can be processed and shipped in the next day's mail. Simply call toll free 1-800-521-6797, (Michigan residents call collect 0-313-477-1850).

3. OUR SERVICE . . . Home Planners makes every effort to process and ship each order for blueprints and books within 48 hours. Because of this, we have deemed it unnecessary to acknowledge receipt of our customers orders. See order coupon for the postage and handling charges for surface mail, air mail or foreign mail.

4. A NOTE REGARDING REVERSE BLUE-PRINTS . . . As a special service to those wishing to build in reverse of the plan as shown, we do include an extra set of reversed blueprints for only $30.00 additional with each order. Even though the lettering and dimensions appear backward on reversed blueprints, they make a handy reference because they show the house just as it's being built in reverse from the standard blueprints — thereby helping you visualize the home better.

5. OUR EXCHANGE POLICY . . . Since blueprints are printed up in specific response to your individual order, we cannot honor requests for refunds. However, the first set of blueprints in any order (or the one set in a single set order) for a given design may be exchanged for a set of another design at a fee of $20.00 plus $3.00 for postage and handling via surface mail; $4.00 via air mail.

How many sets of blueprints should be ordered?

This question is often asked. The answer can range anywhere from 1 to 8 sets, depending upon circumstances. For instance, a single set of blueprints of your favorite design is sufficient to study the house in greater detail. On the other hand, if you are planning to get cost estimates, or if you are planning to build, you may need as many as eight sets of blueprints. Because the first set of blueprints in each order is $125.00, and because additional sets of the same design in each order are only $30.00 each (and with package sets even more economical), you save considerably by ordering your total requirements now. To help you determine the exact number of sets, please refer to the handy check list.

How Many Blueprints Do You Need?

—OWNER'S SET(S)

—BUILDER (Usually requires at least 3 sets: 1 as legal document; 1 for inspection; and at least 1 for tradesmen — usually more.)

—BUILDING PERMIT (Sometimes 2 sets are required.)

—MORTGAGE SOURCE (Usually 1 set for a conventional mortgage; 3 sets for F.H.A. or V.A. type mortgages.)

—SUBDIVISION COMMITTEE (If any.)

—TOTAL NO. SETS REQUIRED

Blueprint Ordering Hotline –

Phone toll free: 1-800-521-6797.
Orders received by 11 a.m. (Detroit time) will be processed the same day and shipped to you the following day. Use of this line restricted to blueprint ordering only. Michigan residents simply call collect 0-313-477-1850.

Kindly Note: When ordering by phone, please state Order Form Key No. located in box at lower left corner of blueprint order form.

In Canada Mail To:
Home Planners, Inc., 20 Cedar St. North
Kitchener, Ontario N2H 2W8
Phone: (519) 743-4169

TO: **HOME PLANNERS, INC., 23761 RESEARCH DRIVE FARMINGTON HILLS, MICHIGAN 48024**

Please rush me the following:

____ SET(S) BLUEPRINTS FOR DESIGN NO(S). _____ $_____
Single Set, $125.00; Additional Identical Sets in Same Order $30.00 ea.
4 Set Package of Same Design, $175.00 (Save $40.00) 8 Set Package of Same Design, $225.00 (Save ($110.00) Material Lists & Specification Outline included.

____ SPECIFICATION OUTLINES @ $3.00 EACH . . . . $_____

____ DETAIL SETS @ $12.95 ea. or both @ $19.95: ☐ PLUMBING ☐ELECTRICAL $_____

Michigan Residents add 4% sales tax $_____

FOR POSTAGE AND HANDLING PLEASE CHECK ✔ & REMIT	☐	$3.00 Added to Order for Surface Mail (UPS) – Any Mdse.
	☐	$4.00 Added for Priority Mail of One-Three Sets of Blueprints.
	☐	$6.00 Added for Priority Mail of Four or more Sets of Blueprints.
	☐	For Canadian orders add $2.00 to above applicable rates.

$_____

☐ C.O.D. PAY POSTMAN (C.O.D. Within U.S.A. Only)

TOTAL in U.S.A. funds $_____

PLEASE PRINT
Name _____
Street _____
City _____ State _____ Zip _____

CREDIT CARD ORDERS ONLY: Fill in the boxes below   Prices subject to change without notice

Credit Card No. [ ][ ][ ][ ][ ][ ][ ][ ][ ][ ][ ][ ][ ][ ][ ][ ]   Expiration Date Month/Year [ ][ ][ ][ ]

CHECK ONE: ☐ VISA ☐ MasterCard
Order Form Key CV6BP
Your Signature _____

BLUEPRINT ORDERS SHIPPED WITHIN 48 HOURS OF RECEIPT!

TO: **HOME PLANNERS, INC., 23761 RESEARCH DRIVE FARMINGTON HILLS, MICHIGAN 48024**

Please rush me the following:

____ SET(S) BLUEPRINTS FOR DESIGN NO(S). _____ $_____
Single Set, $125.00; Additional Identical Sets in Same Order $30.00 ea.
4 Set Package of Same Design, $175.00 (Save $40.00) 8 Set Package of Same Design, $225.00 (Save $110.00) Material Lists & Specification Outline included.

____ SPECIFICATION OUTLINES @ $3.00 EACH . . . . $_____

____ DETAIL SETS @ $12.95 ea. or both @ $19.95: ☐ PLUMBING ☐ELECTRICAL $_____

Michigan Residents add 4% sales tax $_____

FOR POSTAGE AND HANDLING PLEASE CHECK ✔ & REMIT	☐	$3.00 Added to Order for Surface Mail (UPS) – Any Mdse.
	☐	$4.00 Added for Priority Mail of One-Three Sets of Blueprints.
	☐	$6.00 Added for Priority Mail of Four or more Sets of Blueprints.
	☐	For Canadian orders add $2.00 to above applicable rates.

$_____

☐ C.O.D. PAY POSTMAN (C.O.D. Within U.S.A. Only)

TOTAL in U.S.A. funds $_____

PLEASE PRINT
Name _____
Street _____
City _____ State _____ Zip _____

CREDIT CARD ORDERS ONLY: Fill in the boxes below   Prices subject to change without notice

Credit Card No. [ ][ ][ ][ ][ ][ ][ ][ ][ ][ ][ ][ ][ ][ ][ ][ ]   Expiration Date Month/Year [ ][ ][ ][ ]

CHECK ONE: ☐ VISA ☐ MasterCard
Order Form Key CV6BP
Your Signature _____

Design 122920
3,067 Sq. Ft. - First Floor
648 Sq. Ft. - Second Floor; 67,881 Cu. Ft.

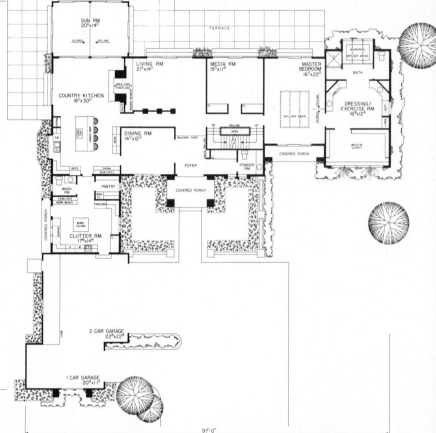

This contemporary design also has a great deal to offer. Study the living areas. A fireplace opens up to both the living room and country kitchen. Privacy is the key word when describing the sleeping areas. The first floor master bedroom is away from the traffic of the house and features a dressing/exercise room, whirlpool tub and shower and a spacious walk-in closet. Two more bedrooms and a full bath are the second floor. The three-car garage is arranged so that the owners have use of a double-garage with an attached single on reserve for guests. The cheerful sunroom adds 296 sq. ft. and 3,789 cu. ft. to the above totals.

TWO-STORY LIVABILITY . . . .

is presented briefly here in its most highly recognizable and popular form - the full two-story. These designs represent a few popular exterior styles. It is but a sampling of over 300 additional full two story designs in the Home Planners, Inc. portfolio. For further information about the availability of the TWO STORY HOMES book kindly turn to page 118. A study and comparison of the designs in the 1½ and two-story homes books will lead to a fuller appreciation and understanding of the two types of designs which so effectively provide outstanding two-level livability for the growing, active family. Such a study will help assure the correct choice of a design as your new home.

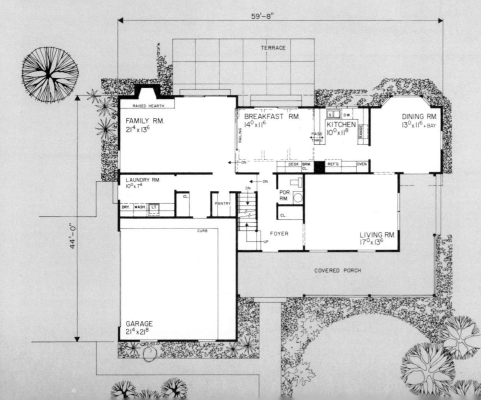

Design 122774

1,370 Sq. Ft. - First Floor
969 Sq. Ft. - Second Floor
38,305 Cu. Ft.

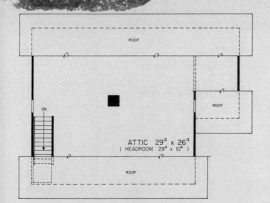

● Here is a Farmhouse adaptation with all the most up-to-date features expected in a new home. Beginning with the formal areas, this design offers pleasures for the entire family. There is the quiet corner living room which has an opening to the sizeable dining room. This room will enjoy plenty of natural light from the delightful bay window overlooking the rear yard. It is also conveniently located with the efficient U-shaped kitchen just a step away. The kitchen features many built-ins with pass-thru to the beamed ceiling breakfast room. Sliding glass doors to the terrace are fine attractions in both the sunken family room and breakfast room. The service entrance to the garage is flanked by a clothes closet and a large, walk-in pantry. There is a secondary entrance thru the laundry room. Recreational activities and hobbies can be pursued in the basement area. Four bedrooms, two baths upstairs.

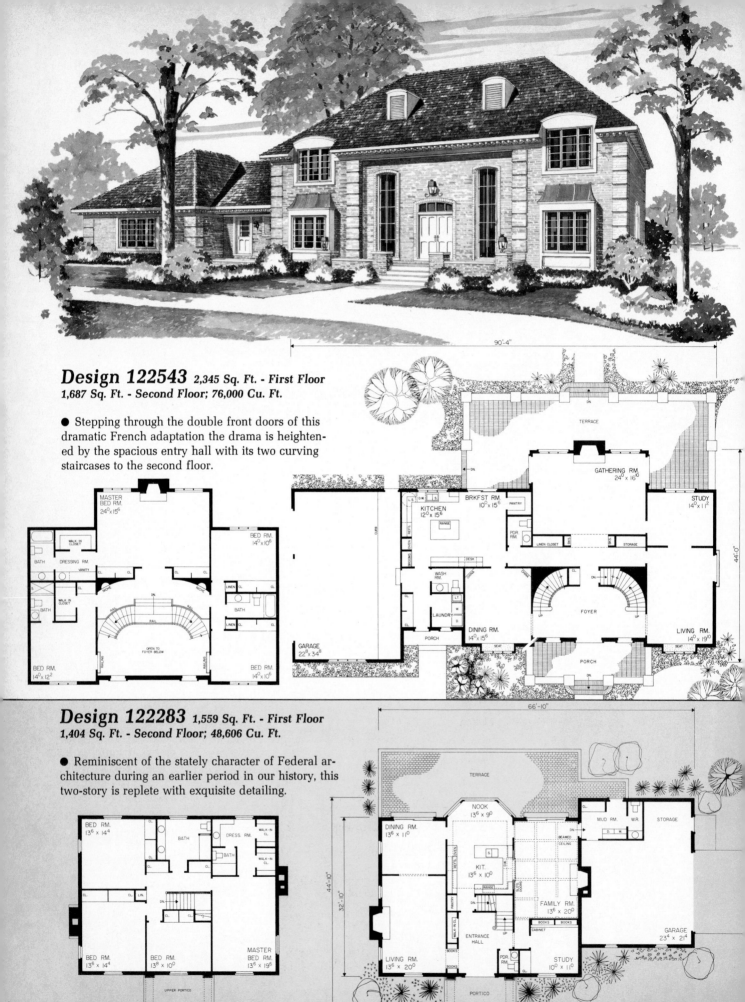

Design 122543 2,345 Sq. Ft. - First Floor
1,687 Sq. Ft. - Second Floor; 76,000 Cu. Ft.

● Stepping through the double front doors of this dramatic French adaptation the drama is heightened by the spacious entry hall with its two curving staircases to the second floor.

90'-4"

MASTER BED RM. 24⁰ x 15⁶

BED RM. 14⁰ x 10⁶

WALK-IN CLOSET

BATH

DRESSING RM.
VANITY

NICHE

NICHE

CL

CL

WALK-IN CLOSET

BATH

LINEN CL

BATH

LINEN CL

DN

RAIL

OPEN TO FOYER BELOW

RAILING

RAILING

BED RM. 14⁰ x 12²

BED RM. 14⁰ x 10⁶

TERRACE

DN

DN

GATHERING RM. 24⁰ x 16⁶

STUDY 14⁰ x 11²

KITCHEN 12⁰ x 15⁶

BRKFST RM. 10⁰ x 15⁶

PANTRY

RANGE

PDR. RM.

LINEN CLOSET

BKS

BKS

STORAGE

CURB

OVEN

REF S

DESK

RANGE

WASH RM.

LT

CL

W

D

CL

CL

CABINET

CL

DN

FOYER

UP

UP

LAUNDRY

GARAGE 22⁸ x 34⁸

PORCH

DINING RM. 14⁰ x 15⁰

SEAT

LIVING RM. 14⁰ x 19¹⁰

SEAT

44'-0"

PORCH

DN

Design 122283 1,559 Sq. Ft. - First Floor
1,404 Sq. Ft. - Second Floor; 48,606 Cu. Ft.

● Reminiscent of the stately character of Federal architecture during an earlier period in our history, this two-story is replete with exquisite detailing.

66'-10"

TERRACE

BED RM. 13⁶ x 14⁴

BATH

DRESS. RM.

WALK-IN CL

WALK-IN CL

CL

CL

BATH

CL

CL

CL

LIN.

DN

CL

CL

BED RM. 13⁶ x 14⁴

BED RM. 13⁸ x 10⁰

MASTER BED RM. 13⁶ x 19⁶

UPPER PORTICO

NOOK 13⁶ x 9⁰

DINING RM. 13⁶ x 11⁰

MUD RM.

W.R.

STORAGE

BEAMED CEILING

D W

REF S

DISH

KIT. 13⁶ x 10⁰

RANGE

FAMILY RM. 13⁶ x 20⁰

GARAGE 23⁴ x 21⁴

WALK-IN CL

DN

BOOKS

BOOKS

BOOKS

CABINET

44'-10"

32'-10"

ENTRANCE HALL

UP

LIVING RM. 13⁶ x 20⁰

PDR. RM.

STUDY 10⁰ x 11⁰

PORTICO

Design 122356 1,969 Sq. Ft. - First Floor
1,702 Sq. Ft. - Second Floor; 55,105 Cu. Ft.

● Here is truly an exquisite Tudor adaptation. Inside, the drama really begins to unfold as one envisions his family's living patterns. The delightfully large receiving hall has a two-story ceiling and controls the flexible traffic patterns.

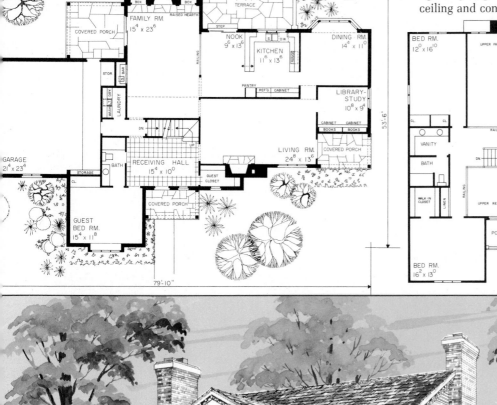

FAMILY RM.
15⁴ x 23⁶

COVERED PORCH

WOOD BOX   WOOD BOX
RAISED HEARTH

TERRACE

STEP

NOOK
9⁶ x 13⁶

KITCHEN
11⁶ x 13⁶

DINING RM.
14⁴ x 11⁰

STOR.

LAUNDRY
WASH'R DRY'R

PANTRY

REF'G.   CABINET

LIBRARY-STUDY
10⁸ x 9⁰

CABINET

CABINET   CABINET
BOOKS   BOOKS

GARAGE
21⁴ x 23⁴

STORAGE

BATH

DN

UP

RECEIVING HALL
15⁴ x 10⁰

GUEST CLOSET

LIVING RM.
24⁸ x 13⁶

COVERED PORCH

CL.

GUEST BED RM.
15⁴ x 11⁸

COVERED PORCH

79'-10"

53'-6"

BED RM.
12⁰ x 16¹⁰

UPPER FAMILY RM.

BED RM.
11⁰ x 14⁰

DRESSING RM.

ROOF

CL.   CL.

LINEN   BATH

BATH

CL.

VANITY

BATH

RAILING

DN

RAILING

CL.

LOUNGE
8⁰ x 10⁰

MASTER BED RM.
18⁰ x 14⁰

ROOF

WALK IN CLOSET

LINEN

UPPER RECEIVING HALL

STORAGE

ROOF

PORCH ROOF

BED RM.
16² x 13⁰

Design 122585
990 Sq. Ft. - First Floor
1,011 Sq. Ft. - Second Floor; 30,230 Cu. Ft.

● A traditional Colonial, a stately Tudor and an elegant French facade house this two-story floor plan. The exteriors are highlighted with large paned-glass windows. Note that the second floor overhangs in the front to extend the size of the master bedroom. After entering through the front door one can either go directly to the formal area or to the informal area.

Design 122586
984 Sq. Ft. - First Floor
1,003 Sq. Ft. - Second Floor; 30,080 Cu. Ft.

● The formal area consists of the living and dining rooms. These two areas stretch from the front to the rear of the house. Together they offer the correct setting for the most formal occasion. The informal area is the front family room. A fireplace will warm this casual, family living area. The work center is easily accessible from all areas, including the garage and terrace.

Design 122587
984 Sq. Ft. - First Floor
993 Sq. Ft. - Second Floor; 30,090 Cu. Ft.

● The second floor has been designed to please all of the family. Four good-sized bedrooms, plenty of closet space and two baths are available. Not a bit of wasted space will be found in these sleeping facilities. Choose your favorite facade to go with this floor plan. Order Design 122585 for the Colonial; Design 122586 for the Tudor and for the French, order Design 122587.